PLANNING FOR FINANCIAL INDEPENDENCE

PLANNING FOR FINANCIAL INDEPENDENCE
Choose your lifestyle   Secure your future

Duncan S. Goheen, B.A., M.S.

Self-Counsel Press
(a division of)
International Self-Counsel Press Ltd.
Vancouver
Toronto   Seattle

Printed in Canada

First edition: March, 1988; Reprinted: August, 1989

Canadian Cataloguing in Publication Data

Goheen, Duncan, 1943-
    Planning for financial independence
    (Self-counsel series)
    Originally published by Leading Edge Publications in 1986, under title, Financial planning for Canadians.
    ISBN 0-88908-672-9
    1. Finance, Personal. 2. Financial security. 3. Estate planning.
I. Title. II. Title: Financial planning for Canadians. III. Series.
HG179.G65 1988   332.024   C88-091060-7

Self-Counsel Press
(a division of)
International Self-Counsel Press Ltd.
1481 Charlotte Road
North Vancouver, British Columbia, V7J 1H1

CONTENTS

APPENDIXES

LIST OF FIGURES

LIST OF TABLES

LIST OF WORKSHEETS

NOTICE TO READERS

Laws are constantly changing. Every effort is made to keep this publication as current as possible. However, neither the author nor the publisher can accept any responsibility for changes to the law or practice that occur after the printing of this publication. Please be sure that you have the most recent edition.

PREFACE

Competition for our time and attention is intense. We all have many responsibilities, things we have to do, things we want to do, and things we ought to do but never get around to. The consequences of putting off some things, however, can be very undesireable — opportunites lost, unnecessary personal hardship, failure of a worthy project, or an unrealized inheritance.

In the final analysis, the quality of our own personal stewardship of our resources has profound consequences for us and for others in our local and global family. Wise resource management is imperative at all levels and our personl financial situation is the level that each of us is most responsible for and most able to do something about.

The objective of this book is to make it easier for you to balance and meet your personal, family, and community (local and global) financial needs in the short run and the long run. Now it's up to you.

This book may be used in several ways. It can be read through to gain an understanding of basic investment concepts, or it can be used as a checklist while dealing with your financial advisors. It is also designed to be used as your personal planning workbook. Part I provides an overview; Part II is an introduction to financial tools; and Part III takes you through the process of creating a personal financial plan one step at a time.

Financial planning professionals can build seminars, workshops, and study courses around this book, or they can be used as an integral part of the consulting process. It is an indispensable part of my own financial planning practice and provides the working text of my planning seminars.

Many of the investment strategies outlined can be affected by changes in government policies. It is, therefore, very important that you keep informed of changes in tax law and other legislation that will affect your financial future. One of the easiest ways to do this is to obtain an annual personal tax planning guide which is available from all of the national accounting firms.

At the same time, the laws relating to compulsory retirement are undergoing analysis by various groups and can be expected to change in the future, emphasizing the necessity of making good financial plans now to achieve financial independence before voluntary retirement.

This book represents many years of research and analysis; but it is a product of the combined efforts of my wife, Madeline, who typed the manuscript; my son, Sam, who did the computer graphics; Don (Hippo) Nicholson, who was involved in updating information; Stephen Osborne, who guided the project from concept to finished product; and Roman Evancic who made detailed reviews of the work as it progressed. My thanks to them all.

PART I
PERSONAL FINANCIAL PLANNING

This book is about "financial independence:" a phrase that can mean different things to different people. To some it suggests inherited wealth; to others, getting rich suddenly by winning the lottery perhaps, or making a successful speculation in real estate.

To me, financial independence means, quite simply, being able to choose — especially being able to choose whether or not to work at a job, or to go on a journey, or to stay at home and — say — write a book. I think of financial independence as a desirable condition: a condition worth achieving as part of my overall life plan. In fact, financial independence is a crucial part of my plan for living a full life for as long as I can.

Planning to achieve financial independence means planning for your whole life: establishing a standard of living adequate to the lifestyle you prefer and maintaining that standard through retirement and old age. There can be no simple definition of "adequate standard" here; it is simply a function of each of our different lives.

A financial plan can be no better than the life plan it reflects. To the extent that goals in your life plans are hazy and ill formed, any financial planning you might do will necessarily be hazy and ill formed as well, and probably inappropriate.

Sound financial and life planning requires that you carefully consider your personal values and beliefs. What is it that is really important to you as an individual? What do you see as the purpose of your personal and professional life? From the answers to these questions, you can derive goals at various times in your life.

Once your goals are established, you can make the plans to achieve them and begin to include in your life the rewarding activities of reviewing and managing your plans for living. A financial plan is a part of this overall process.

Planning for your life requires that you think about the future. This is not the image of life that you find in the popular media with its heavy emphasis on the illusion of eternal youth and living only for the present. But planning for your life financially means developing an understanding of how closely today's spending and saving decisions are linked to tomorrow's spending needs. How you live tomorrow depends directly on the decisions you make today, and often you do not even realize that you are making decisions at all.

If you are not yet retired or of retirement age, you will want to make your financial plan with retirement in mind. You will want to achieve financial independence by the time you reach that age.

If you are retired now, ask yourself if you are financially independent: that is, will you be able to maintain the standard of living you desire for the rest of your life. (In this age, the "rest of your life" is likely to be a much longer time than you think.) If the answer is no, then it's time to take appropriate action to rectify that situation. It is never too late to make a life plan.

THE ESSENTIAL QUESTION

The essential planning question, for young and old, can be put fairly simply: how much money (or capital) do you need to achieve financial independence by a specific date, given the standard of living that you desire?

What is the best way for you to accumulate the capital you require, and what is the most tax effective way for you to convert your capital into income, as you require it?

This book will help you address these questions as well as give you the tools you need to create a future course to follow. It is designed to enable you to review your present capital accumulation and insurance programs in light of your future objectives and to help you decide whether or not changes are required. If you do not have a financial program, this book will be your guide to creating one.

This book is aimed at "futureproofing" a standard of living for yourself and (if it is part of your life plan) for your dependents.

RETIREMENT: A MODERN PHENOMENON

Retirement as we know it today was first institutionalized more than 100 years ago in Germany. It was General Bismarck who, as part of his social reform program, set the retirement age at 65 and established pensions to begin then. At the time this was a very conservative innovation, and not very expensive, because 100 years ago the average life expectancy was about 48. While the Bismarck Plan remains essentially intact in most western democracies today, conditions of life have changed drastically.

Life expectancies have increased more than threefold over the last 2,000 years. One hundred years ago the few men who reached age 65 could expect to live just a few more years: a woman perhaps a couple of years longer. Today a man and woman aged 65 may conservatively plan to live to 81 and 87, respectively. These considerably extended lifetimes have drastically altered the economics of the Bismarck Plan and have rendered it nearly impractical. Simply, too many of us are living for far too long.

It is longevity that people so frequently fail to take into account in their personal plans. Time is always of the essence in any financial plan. If, for example, you have made a budget for the next eight months and proceed to carry it out, you don't want to learn in the seventh month that you are going to have to stretch the budget over a twelve-month period. But this is essentially what happens to many retired people — they miscalculate their life expectancies.

Inflation is another contemporary condition that acts as a function of time and can seriously affect any planning for the future. At an annual inflation rate of 5%, the purchasing power of the dollar will drop by one-half every 14 years. The effects can be dramatic. If you retire at age 60, you will see the purchasing power of each dollar cut in half by age 74. Each dollar of savings will have "depreciated" by 50%. A fixed pension can be effectively wiped out during your retirement by nothing more than the inexorable process of inflation.

As an example, consider the story of a railroad pensioner who, in 1953, went on a full pension of $16 per month. In 1953, $16 had the purchasing power of about $83 in 1988. Inflation, as well as our new longevity, has made the Bismarck Plan, on its own, no longer workable in our society.

Many people look to government and corporate pension plans for their future security. But herein lies false hope. The pension benefits that these plans entitle you to are frequently insufficient to meet living expenses. Furthermore, pension money has to come from somewhere, and currently the government's unfunded liability on current pension programs far exceeds the national debt. In 1986, the U.S. unfunded pension liability was estimated to be more than $4 trillion. The Reagan administration has taken steps to reduce its pension obligations, and the present Canadian administration is following suit. Both governments are strongly urging employers and individuals to provide for private retirement savings programs. They know the benefits from public programs will be insufficient and must be supplemented.

Company pension plans are themselves often in precarious circumstances. In 1984, for example, the U.S. Railroad Pension Fund was bailed out by the Treasury Department to the tune of $4 billion. Without the bail-out, pension benefits in that plan would have been cut by 50%. Many corporate pension funds are seriously concerned about their ability to continue to pay out full pensions.

With indications like these, you can understand why more and more people are taking their personal futures into their own hands by developing long-range plans for their retirements and for the eventual disposition of their estates. That's what this book is all about.

There are, of course, many examples of successful retirements and most of them are the result of one common factor: the building up of a capital sum large enough to fund the retirement years along with the usual public and private pension programs. There is no secret method; it's simply a matter of developing a personal capital accumulation program over a long time. This means long-term planning and a personal commitment to enacting the plan. For those of you who are now near or in retirement, there are still many avenues open to you by which you can increase the income from your current savings. I strongly advise doing some long-range planning even after you are retired to be sure that your funds do not terminate before you do.

Money and financial planning are the focus of this book. While it is true, of course, that money cannot guarantee happiness, a 50% drop in income can result in a lot of unhappiness in a hurry, as many retired people today will testify. What we believe about retirement and aging is also important to the success of our own retirements. Our culture, with its emphasis on youth, tends to ignore the lives of our older citizens. It is at our own peril that we accept such trends.

Financial independence does not happen by chance. This book is intended as a tool to help you develop your goals and objectives and your financial strategy for a successful, enjoyable life. In the following pages, I first look at the conditions under which you must make your plans for the future. Part II then provides a close look at the financial tools available to you; and in Part III you can work out in detail your own personal plan.

CRITICAL CHALLENGES AND CHANGES

Failure to plan for change is planning for failure. Sensitivity to change in your personal and business life and allowing for these changes in your personal life and financial plans is essential for successful living.

Cellular radio, artificial intelligence, biotechnology, solar and wind generated energy, and accelerated learning and optimum development of human potential are but a few developments that will have a major impact on our socioeconomic environments.

Kenichi Ohmae, in his book *The Mind of the Strategist*, notes that those corporations that are very successful in today's international economy have —

(a) identified the critical success factors in their industry, and

(b) focused on the development of high levels of competency in those areas.

He notes that there are many other areas that these particular companies do not excel in, but that these other areas are not critical to their success. One of the key success factors in successful living today is effective, long-range personal financial planning and management. It is just as important for you as an individual as it is for a corporation to identify your present situation accurately and honestly, specify your goals very clearly, develop an effective plan for accomplishing these goals within a time frame, and then implement and manage the plan with regular updates and reviews of the entire process.

Those who fail to do this cannot possibly cope with change effectively, leaving their lives to be buffeted about like a ship without a rudder. The choice is between long-range planning and hard thinking now in order to avoid trial and error living later; and living by trial and error later in order to avoid some hard thinking now.

Sound financial planning is as important as a lifetime of hard work.

SOME CASE HISTORIES

Let's take a look at some true stories.

Case 1: Dr. A

Dr. A is 68 and married. Dr. A wanted to retire three years ago but is still working. He is very well known in his field both nationally and internationally and has developed leading-edge operating techniques as well as a busy clinic. He is perceived as being very successful by his peers.

As his career evolved, Dr. A regularly invested his available savings in tax-sheltered investments. With the downturn in the economy, he not only lost all of his invested money, but also found himself in a position of liability as a result of letters of personal guarantee that he signed on several of his projects. He is currently in a state of quiet desperation. He is getting older, he is still working a full schedule, he hasn't the energy that he used to have, but he has no capital with which to fund his retirement.

Dr. A is accustomed to a standard of living that would require a retirement income of at least $5,000 a month. He is very bitter about government policies and programs that, in his opinion, have severely jeopardized his investments, but he has no recourse. He will work as long as he can and eventually retire on an income a mere fraction of that which he is accustomed to. Needless to say, neither he nor his wife are looking forward to the day that income from his practice stops.

Mr. B and his wife retired in 1966. They sold their farm for $600,000 which, in current dollars, would be over $2 million. Mr. B considered himself a wealthy man at the time. He moved to an idyllic resort area and purchased a house, a boat, a truck, and several other things that he had always dreamed of; he was very comfortable.

**Case 2:
Mr. and Mrs. B**

Many of his friends and family members needed loans. Mr. B was a generous man and helped them out. When repayment time came, however, friends and family either were unable or did not see fit to repay the loans.

Mr. B began to scale down his standard of living and he bought a smaller home. Eventually, as a result of loan problems and the erosion of his capital due to inflation, he had to move back into the small rural area that he came from. His wife was forced to go out into the marketplace to do house cleaning, and when arthritis finally crippled her joints to the point where she could no longer work, it was necessary for him to begin taking on small jobs and do craft work to meet grocery expenses.

Mr. and Mrs. C are both 69. Five years ago they had a net worth of $4 million. The real estate market in their city was buoyant. They invested heavily in that marketplace and signed guarantees on several projects. Then the economy reversed and the letters of guarantee were called. They did not understand the guarantees they had signed, and neither had they anticipated the reversal in the economy. They lost their investments and today are subsisting on the proceeds of government social assistance programs. Their standard of living has dropped by approximately 90%.

**Case 3:
Mr. and Mrs. C**

Ms. D is 68. She is single and lives alone in an apartment. She worked all her life for the telephone company and is receiving an indexed pension that is currently more than her expenses. She is spending approximately 75% of her income, giving part of it to charity, and saving the balance. She lives a very simple life and travels very little, but does

Case 4: Ms. D

all that she wants to do. She has no financial problems and is able to do as she pleases. The pension fund that she contributed to over her 40 years of service is now providing amply for her modest requirements.

Case 5: Mr. and Mrs. E

Mr. and Mrs. E are 63 and 56, respectively. Mr. E is retired and is earning a disability pension. As a result of a profit-sharing program at work as well as personal savings, they have accumulated approximately $300,000 which they are using to purchase life income annuities. This money, which is supplementing their pension incomes, will provide a very comfortable retirement for them. The only vulnerability is Mrs. E's; if Mr. E. dies, the disability income is lost. Because her life expectancy is still more that 30 years, the savings fund would be insufficient to support her in the lifestyle she desires.

Case 6: Mr. and Mrs. F

Mr. F, 65, and his wife, 60, are now retired. They sold some property at a very handsome profit and now have a net worth in excess of $3 million. After doing a careful long-range budget, bringing inflation into account, Mr. and Mrs. F realized that they required $2 million of this money to generate the income they required through their projected life expectancies. They will secure their future income by purchasing creditor-proof prescribed annuities and blue chip securities with the $2 million, and they will make some higher-risk speculative investments with the remaining $1 million.

Case 7: The Widows G and H

Widows G and H had both been happily married with two and three children respectively. When they and their husbands were in their early forties, both families were enjoying comfortable lifestyles and had considerable real estate assets. One of the husbands died in an accident and the other died of a heart attack.

Widow G is still living quite comfortably, having suffered little change in her lifestyle. Widow H and her children, however, suffered a traumatic reduction in their lifestyle, and they even lost their home.

The difference in the two cases was life insurance. Mr. G had planned well to supply adequate life insurance capital for his survivors, whereas Mr. H had not. Although both estates consisted of real estate, these assets proved to be of little value because of a depressed market and the loss of the husbands themselves, whose management skills and expertise were important to the success of the real estate investments. When Mr. G died, a substantial tax-free, creditor-proof capital sum was paid to his wife by their insurance company. It was this life insurance capital that allowed her and her family to maintain their standard of living.

WHAT WENT WRONG: THE UNSUCCESSFUL CASES

Many unsuccessful retirements result from very unwise tax-shelter investments. Dr. A always made his tax-shelter investments at the eleventh hour and with very little or no research into the underlying economics of the investment. The salespeople he dealt with were very aggressive and assured him that there was little risk to the investment.

They told him what he wanted to hear. He had some reservations about their promises, but because of the pressures of time and his desire to reduce taxes, he went along with them.

Will Rogers once said that when he was younger he was primarily concerned about the return on his investment, but as he grew older he became more and more interested in the return *of* his investment. We have just come through a cycle in our economy in which the experience of Dr. A has been shared by many, not only among professionals, but among the general public as well.

It's very easy in a buoyant economy to get caught up in the "everybody's doing it, everybody's winning" investment strategy, but these cycles always come to an end.

What would Dr. A do if he had to do it over again? He would put his savings into guaranteed interest savings programs and do what he does best, which is focus on his practice. That way he would have accumulated a substantial sum of capital and he would have retired three years ago with a comfortable life income.

His recommendation is that you should consider equities only if you have the time, expertise, and energy to thoroughly research and administer them. But if you are very busy in your day-to-day affairs with your own business, then it is better to have a guaranteed savings and investment program. In his opinion, the only winners in his situation were the people who earned the fees and commissions from the sale of the tax-shelter programs.

Inflation, combined with the lack of a long-term financial plan, resulted in the disasters experienced by Mr. and Mrs. B, the retired farm family. Nobody in 1966 projected that inflation would have reduced the purchasing power of a dollar by 75% by the year 1984.

The retired couple, if you had asked them in 1966, would not have anticipated such a long life span. They also had no long-term plan to fund their total retirement. If they had had a plan in place they would have been much more conservative regarding loans to friends and family.

Inflation has eroded fixed pension incomes as well as accumulations of capital dramatically over the past two decades and will continue to do so over the foreseeable future. It is a problem with no ready answers, and most economists agree that inflation will continue to be a fact of life. Taking inflation into account in the long-term financial planning process is essential. Long-term planning is a process of forecasting income and expenses, taking inflation and interest rates into account, planning the budget, and then managing that plan. Failure to do so is to court disaster.

Most people recognize these principles in business but fail to apply these same time-tested and proven practices in their personal affairs. Mr. and Mrs. B failed to do so and are paying a very heavy penalty as a result.

Once your income ceases, there is very little room for error in the budgeting process. Therefore, it is even more essential to do long-term financial planning in retirement than before retirement. (A step-by-step long-term planning process is outlined in Part III.)

Mr. and Mrs. B's final error was to unwittingly enter into a business in which they had no expertise or background — the business of

7

lending money. If you are depending on funds for your livelihood, it is essential that you take a businesslike approach toward the investment or lending of that money. Mr. and Mrs. B used more heart than head when they loaned money to their friends and family.

Mrs. H and her husband didn't get around to taking a serious look at their capital needs in the event of Mr. H's death. Like many of us, they preferred not to consider the question. Mr. H handled most of the financial decisions, and his wife was inclined not to "interfere." Now a widow, she wishes she had been more involved in the family's finances, particularly with long-range planning. She and her children are now paying the price for their failure to secure themselves financially.

WHAT WENT RIGHT: THE SUCCESSFUL CASES

Ms. D, who worked for 40 years for the telephone company, contributed throughout her lifetime to her pension program. She contributed a small sum each week, but totalled over her lifetime, this amounted to a considerable sum. Fortunately she did not have a problem with portability of her pension, because she was with the same company for her entire career. Another reason for her successful retirement is that her expenses are relatively low. She has not changed her lifestyle appreciably from her working days and, as a result, has a surplus of income over expenses. She is very prudent and cautious with her funds, knows very little about the equity market, and, therefore, stays clear of it.

Mr. and Mrs. F put in many long years of hard work building up real estate assets. Mr. F knew the hospitality industry well and invested and reinvested all his money in it throughout his working days. Every time he made an investment outside of his area of expertise he regretted it. Fortunately only a minority of his funds went astray, and the bulk stayed in the assets that he administered directly from day to day. He sold the assets at the peak of the market and is now financially secure. Mr. and Mrs. F are currently making some equity investments, but they are doing so one step at a time, with the majority of their funds in guaranteed investments. Again, they are very prudent in the use of funds and have not changed their lifestyle significantly, even after the very profitable sale of major assets. From some of the minor negative experiences that they have had with investments, they realize how quickly they could lose what they have spent a lifetime to build up. They have set aside the funds required for a comfortable retirement and placed them in guaranteed investments, and they are using the balance for equity and higher risk investments.

Mrs. E and her husband are similar to Ms. D in that they have worked for a lifetime, saving throughout, and are participating in a company profit-sharing program that is working out well for them. Their savings again have been in the form of guaranteed savings. Approximately 20% of their savings is in equities, which are primarily blue chip stocks.

Mrs. G and her husband, with the help of a good adviser, had made a realistic estimate of the tax-free capital they would need in the event of his death or disability. They took lifestyle, inflation, and life expectancy into account. As a result of this sound planning *and implementation*, Mrs. G and her family have been able to maintain their lifestyle.

In the unsuccessful cases, you can see the effects of having either no plan in place or having an unsuitable plan involving high risk or unfamiliar programs. Even in those cases where people had achieved financial independence, lack of a plan resulted in capital running out part way through retirement.

The successful cases all demonstrate the effectiveness of a sound, long-range plan, both offensive and defensive. These plans were implemented, and when income was needed the capital was available to be converted into income according to a budget designed ahead of time. These successful cases share three aspects of good planning:

(a) Long-range plan and plan implementation for capital accumulation (offensive plan)

(b) Long-range plan and plan implementation for capital to be made available in event of death or disability (defensive plan)

(c) Efficient conversion of capital into income as required by the plan to provide a satisfactory income for life.

Most successful retirees have had a regular savings program throughout their life and/or have reinvested their money in their own businesses or in fields in which they have expertise. People who make investments in areas in which they are unfamiliar often suffer losses.

Significant capital accumulation rarely occurs through tax shelters or get-rich-quick schemes. People who go into retirement with a large sum of capital earned from speculation in stocks or businesses that they knew little or nothing about are extremely rare, and yet huge investments are made each year by many people in such ventures. This is not the way capital is accumulated; it is usually accumulated one step at a time, and it is usually done with guaranteed funds, professionally managed funds, or in businesses in which the investor has considerable expertise and puts in a lot of sweat, time, and energy. The successful retiree only puts at high risk those funds that he or she can afford to do without.

In summary, it pays to be very conservative in your savings and investment program unless you have considerable expertise and experience in the proposed investment. Many people during the last five years have lost their life savings by allowing themselves to be swept up in enthusiasm for big profits being earned by "everyone else." The psychology of sure winnings is an indicator that a downturn is just over the next hill.

There always have been and always will be cycles, seasons, tides, ups and downs, fair weather and foul in the affairs of humans. The acceptance of these events as a normal part of living and the wise preparation for them are key factors in planning for the future. To ignore these cycles and pretend that the sun always shines and will continue to shine 24 hours a day is foolhardy and can result in massive ups and downs in day-to-day living.

People tend to be short-range thinkers and planners in their personal lives. Very little in the way of emergency funds are set aside to carry us through times of unemployment, disability, ill health, loss of life of a key family income earner, etc. Through the advertising media — radio, TV, and newspapers — we have been conditioned to buy now and pay later, let tomorrow look after itself, and maximize our consumption by spending all of today's income and as much of tomorrow's as lenders will finance.

The cost of such a life strategy in financial terms is widespread pension poverty and high levels of privation during working years. Newborn children as well as our eldest citizens all become financial victims.

The psychological and sociological costs are less tangible, but just as real. Anxiety, depression, loss of self-esteem, family breakdowns, and mental and emotional stress have become accepted as a way of life in our culture. This is in no small part due to our unwillingness to accept economic cycles as a normal part of our personal financial lives and to prepare accordingly.

Seventy-five percent of women at some time in their lives will be left to manage their own financial affairs as a result of a separation, divorce, or widowhood. Most of these women are unprepared for the task. Two-thirds of this group over 65 are living below the poverty line. Women receive approximately half as much pension and annuity income as men.

Failure to take personal economic cycles and changing circumstances into account in a basic retirement financial plan is the obvious cause of the problem. In Canada, less than one-third of the nation's self-employed men and women have a private pension plan, and approximately half of those in private industry have a plan. Even those with a plan will at best have their incomes reduced by 40% to 50% when they retire.

Some recent labor/management agreements have included provisions for indexed pensions, but one problem with indexing is that the initial monthly income is substantially lower than with the non-indexed plan. Many people prefer a higher income when they are younger and healthier. If a pension is not indexed, however, and there are no other sources of income or assets that can be converted into income, an economic squeeze can result. For example, the purchasing power of a $500 monthly pension will drop to $250 in 14 years, assuming 5% annual inflation, which would leave pensioners destitute if they achieve normal life expectancy. This leads to the alarming statistic that more than half of our citizens over 65 are living at a minimum subsistence level by North American standards.

LOOKING TO GOVERNMENT

For most people the level of personal income that the government is willing or able to provide is grossly inadequate if there are no other sources of income. Both Canadian and U.S. federal debts are increasing at an alarming rate. You frequently hear boasts by the governing bodies that the rate at which the debt is increasing is slowing down and that the annual deficit is decreasing. But the fact is that the overall debt is rapidly increasing. In your personal and corporate lives this kind of irresponsible financial management may work in the short run, but in the long run it is disastrous. It also does not work for a nation.

There is a direct trade-off between our current and future consumption; if we consume more now, there will be less consumption later and

10

vice versa. Our governments, however, do not seem to balance this trade-off in a responsible way.

The Canadian and U.S. annual deficits as a percentage of gross national product (GNP) more than doubled from 1975 to 1985. (See Figure #1.) The federal debt as a percentage of GNP increased from 23% to 36% in Canada and from 28% to 40% in the United States over the same period. (See Figure #2.) The rapidly escalating debt results in even more severe increases in annual debt charges: from $1.9 billion to $21.7 billion annually in Canada and from $26.7 billion to $142.7 billion annually in the United States from 1975 to 1985. (See Figure #3.)

FIGURE #1
CANADIAN/U.S. ANNUAL DEFICITS
(as a percentage of GNP)

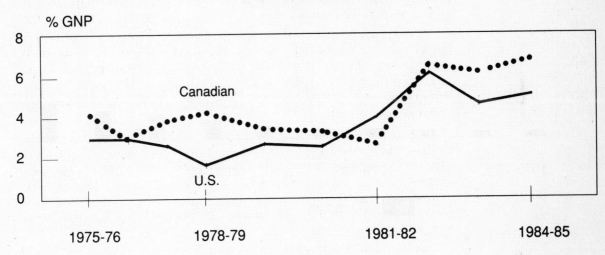

FIGURE #2
CANADIAN/U.S. DEBT
(as a percentage of GNP)

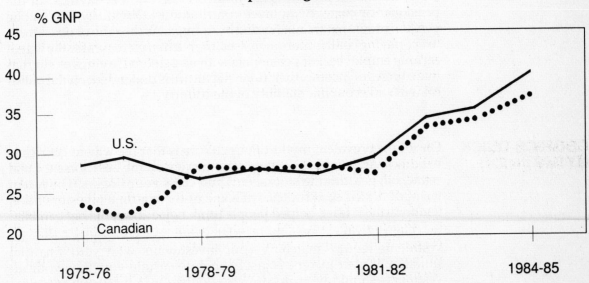

11

FIGURE #3
CANADIAN/U.S. ANNUAL DEBT CHARGES

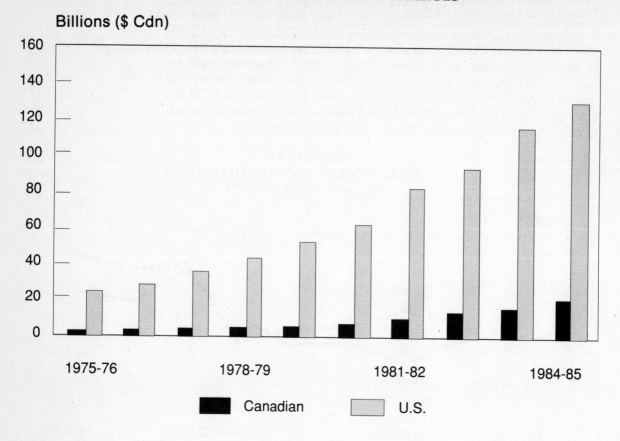

Billions ($ Cdn)

■ Canadian   ☐ U.S.

Government-controlled pension plans are rapidly running short of funds. Either public pension contributions will have to be markedly increased or the pension income decreased for the programs to remain solvent. Pension programs are funded either by the "savings" of the pensioner or current employee contributions. Obviously, our public pension programs are not funded by savings. As the ratio of pensioners to tax-paying contributors increases, the burden increases for the wage-earning employee. For pensioners with no personal savings or alternative sources of income, their financial future is dependent on the political will and economic stability of the country.

GET-RICH-QUICK MYTHS

One of the prevalent myths of our culture is that the way to get rich is to be a clever gambler — to put your money on the best horse (or real estate, oil, gas, mining stocks, etc.) and cross your fingers. The recent well-publicized bankruptcies of some of the big time investors have, temporarily at least, helped people think twice about the big gamble.

"Get rich quick" usually translates into "get poor quick." Risk investments require matching your investments with your financial situation. If your income is just enough to sustain you, then your investments should be in secure areas only. Once you have sufficient

12

capital to generate an income that provides for your current basic needs and for the rest of your life, you will then be in a position to consider high risk investments, if they are attractive to you.

Risk investment must be approached very cautiously. First, who are you doing business with? Do you know their track record? Have they any experience in the field? Do they have the capital they will need? Have they the management expertise or the technical knowledge to make the venture a success?

Eight characteristics of any investment are —

(a) risk,

(b) return,

(c) liquidity,

(d) cash flow,

(e) term,

(f) inflation protection,

(g) tax benefits, and

(h) management effort.

Risks include —

(a) the possibility that interest rates in general will change, causing an adverse change in an investor's return on the market value of his or her assets

(b) the market risk that the demand for the investor's assets will fall, bringing down the market value of the assets

(c) the purchasing power risk that inflation will erode much of the real value of the investor's asset so that when it is sold, the purchasing power of the proceeds may not have kept pace with inflation during the term of the investment

(d) the psychological risk that the investor may make impulsive, poorly timed investment decisions.

It is very important to match risk with an investor's expertise, temperament, and interest.

The potential return on an investment is usually directly related to the degree of risk of the investment. Returns may be in the form of capital gains or income which includes interest, dividends, rent, or profits. The riskier the investment, the higher the expected return, but also the greater the chance of receiving a low or negative return.

Liquidity refers to the ability and time required to convert an investment to cash without loss of principal. Investments that are highly liquid often have lower returns than others.

Cash flow relates to the timing and amount of the investment return (and any associated debt payments). Do you require immediate cash flow or can you leave the investment in place for long-term capital appreciation without the benefit of current cash flow?

The term of an investment is the length of time to its maturity. Investors need to know if the investment is locked in until a specific time and how their return will be affected if they hold the investment for only a short time. As the term of an investment increases, the return also usually increases.

Inflation protection is particularly important for long-term investments. Some years ago many investors were buying low-yielding long-term bonds (before inflation became a chronic problem). As these bonds mature, the holders are receiving back the full amount of the principal, but its purchasing power is only a small fraction of what it was when the bonds were issued. Common stocks and real estate have historically provided protection against inflation because of their capital appreciation, but there have been periods when they depreciated severely.

Tax benefits are important, especially if the investor is in a medium or high tax bracket. The tax treatment of different types of investments has a large impact on the after-tax returns available to individual investors.

Management effort is another important investment characteristic. Do you have the time, energy, and inclination, as well as the expertise to select and manage your investment, or do you want to have a hands-off, trouble-free investment?

Each of these characteristics must be carefully weighed and considered for each investor.

With income and/or equity-based tax sheltered investments, investors are frequently aware of the benefits of the investment performing equal to or better than the financial projections, but are often unaware of the consequences of the investment falling short of the projections.

Make sure that you know the tax, equity, and income/expense consequences of all scenarios and be prepared to live with them. The psychology of winning is infectious in times of economic prosperity and most people do not prepare for the worst.

Srully Blotnik, in his book *Getting Rich Your Own Way*, studied 1,500 Americans from 1960 to 1980. Of the 1,000 he managed to keep track of, 83 became millionaires. He searched for a common denominator and found that they spent very little time and effort looking for or making investments of a speculative nature outside of their own areas of expertise. If they did, their investments were very secure. Blotnik's book clearly refutes many common beliefs and assumptions about "how to make a million."

STOCKS, BONDS, AND FUTURES MARKET

The financial marketplace is changing at an unprecedented rate. The financial controls available to federal regulatory bodies have never been less effective than they are today. In fact, the chairman of the New York Stock Exchange, in a speech given in Toronto in September, 1987, spoke of the very real possibility of a "financial meltdown" in the marketplace because of the lack of effective regulatory controls by federal bodies (*The Globe and Mail*, September 28, 1987).

Almost everyone has been on the "equity bandwagon" over the past few years. Most technical analysts agree that sharp corrections (rapidly falling prices) will occur in the marketplace within the next two years. Most unsophisticated investors, which make up the largest group of investors, climb on this bandwagon near the end of a rising cycle, hang on for too long during a major correction, and then bail out after losing a substantial portion of their capital.

Make sure that you establish your selling price position the minute you buy. Most investors do not do this and eventually regret not following this basic rule.

While it is true that over the long run equities outperform guaranteed interest rates of return, it is also true that most unsophisticated investors do not stay in the market over the long run. Watch the next market downturn and carefully observe investor behavior.

TIME, INFLATION, AND INTEREST

The first thing to be determined in any financial planning process is the period to be planned for. Planning to fund ten years of living expenses is of little use if, in fact, one lives an extra five years.

Similarly, if you assume that an income-reducing event will not happen for fifteen years and it happens in five years, and you have not prepared for such an eventuality, the consequences can be equally disastrous. Most people today are doing retirement planning with the assumption that they are going to live be 70 or 75 years. But as the table in Appendix 1 shows, the life expectancy estimate for a 65-year-old male or female Canadian is 80 and 84 years respectively. Further, many actuaries are using estimates of 81 and 87 years. In the interests of being conservative, I have used the latter estimates here.

As well, income earners who assume that they will be healthy and able to work and to fulfill their income-producing objectives but become disabled due to health or accident can also experience severe financial consequences. Similarly, the death of a key income earner prior to the time that has been anticipated, without provision having been made for such a situation, can be disastrous for the family survivors. Time is a critical factor, whether it's in retirement or any other stage in adult life. The actuaries' statistics are important to the life planner.

Morbidity information is also available. Figures compiled this decade indicate that rates of hospitalization per 1,000 population averaged around 150 with 20% of the group aged 45 to 64. Appendix 2 shows the total number of patient days spent in hospitals by sex and by major causes for the year 1980 to 1981.

Until you reach an advanced age, you are more likely to become disabled than to die. For example, if you are 30, your chances of disability for 90 days or more versus death are 2.7 to 1. If you are 40, the ratio is 2.3 to 1; if you are 50, 1.8 to 1; and if you are 59, 1.6 to 1.

The chances of becoming disabled are far higher than most people realize. Out of an average group of income earners between the ages of 25 and 45, disability due to sickness or accident will occur with the following approximate frequencies and durations:

1 out of 3 will have a loss of earning power for 6 months.

1 out of 4 will have a loss of earning power for 1 year.

1 out of 5 will have a loss of earning power for 2 years.

1 out of 7 will have a loss of earning power for 5 years.

Inflation over time is also essential information to incorporate in a good personal financial plan. Failure to take inflation into account can have very negative consequences, particularly for those on fixed incomes who have outlived their money.

COORDINATED PLANS

Most of us could use the services of lawyers, accountants, bankers, life insurance agents, stock brokers, realtors, etc., much more effectively and efficiently. There could frequently be much better coordination among the professional team, resulting in the reduction of fragmented and sometimes contradictory steps that each of the team members may take when acting independently. The professional can do a much better job for the client if he or she knows where the client wants to go in the long run, and when he or she wants to get there.

Many professionals are not long-range planners, but require the direction that comes from such a plan. Once this is in place, professionals can complement each other and strengthen the efforts of other professional assistance.

THE TWO MAJOR PHASES OF A PERSONAL FINANCIAL PLAN

The two major phases of each financial plan are —

(a) from now to retirement, and

(b) from the beginning to the end of retirement.

Both of these phases in turn have two major components. The first is the offensive strategy, that is, the plan to generate sufficient income and capital to fund living expenses and accomplish other financial objectives throughout your lifetime. The second component is the defensive strategy, which is taking the necessary measures to avoid or adequately cope with potential adversities encountered through economic cycles and life in general.

FROM NOW TO RETIREMENT: AN OFFENSIVE STRATEGY

This part of the plan requires an in-depth analysis of your current position in terms of income, expenses, assets, and liabilities. It also involves a detailed definition and statement of your financial goals. What standard of living do you want between now and retirement? What are your financial requirements for education, travel, leisure activities, etc.?

Detailed projections of anticipated income will also be made. After this has been done, the third step is to determine the most effective plan for producing the income required, not only to fund living expenses between now and retirement but also to generate the capital required to fund the standard of living desired during retirement.

FROM NOW TO RETIREMENT: A DEFENSIVE STRATEGY

Death, disability, unemployment, business failure, and emergency health requirements are but a few of the common adversities that must be considered in a personal financial plan.

Death

In the event of the death of an income earner or provider of household and mothering services, an adequate insurance program needs to be in place to fund the income loss and/or purchase the services that were formerly rendered. It is common to insure cars, homes, etc. at the level required to repair or replace them. For life insurance, the calculations required to determine the amount of coverage needed are much more complex. By means of " what-if " scenarios, it is possible to determine the capital sum required to protect a family income for a given number of years, and/or to replace services rendered, given interest rate and inflation assumptions. (See Appendix 3.) (Table #5 on page 53 shows an example illustrating the amount of insurance required to provide a family income for various time intervals.)

One of the most common errors when determining types of insurance, once the amount has been established, is using an overly simplistic approach. To determine the pros and cons of term versus permanent insurance, you must do economic projections over your entire life expectancy. An added value of permanent insurance that many analysts have neglected is the significantly increased pension income that results from having personal permanent insurance in place for life. This added income is the result of selecting a single life instead of joint life pension income.

The added income can be as much as 20% higher, which, throughout a retirement life span, can be significant. This benefit should be considered when comparing term and permanent insurance. (See Table #6 in Part II to compare the costs of term and permanent insurance.)

Table #1 below illustrates the difference between single and joint life annuity payments.

TABLE #1
COMPARISON OF SINGLE LIFE AND JOINT LIFE ANNUITY PAYMENTS*

Male age	Female age	Annual payments from $100,000 annuity	
		Single life (male) no guarantee	Joint life no guarantee
65	65	$12,904.23	$11,145.57
65	60	12,904.23	10,854.85
65	55	12,904.23	10,604.78
65	50	12,904.23	10,398.75

*Based on rates currently offered by a large insurance company.

Emergency funds

Emergency funds must be available to provide for times of unemployment, unexpected medical bills, unanticipated house repairs, maintenance, etc. An emergency reserve that will fund six months of normal living expenses is normally adequate. A modest amount of cash is required if other assets are available that can be readily converted into cash, and, of course, this amount also depends on the disability income insurance you have in place. Disability insurance that generates non-taxable income at the rate of 65% to 70% of your anticipated income for the duration of your anticipated working life will reduce the required emergency fund considerably. Part of determining your position in terms of income, expenses, assets and liabilities, includes a very careful analysis of your insurance program.

Make sure that your emergency fund is able to carry you through until such time as disability insurance takes effect. If you are in a highly volatile business and economic downturns either reduce your income considerably or have the potential of putting you out of business, then, of course, the emergency reserves need to increase. The same is true for people employed in seasonal occupations. In these cases you need to determine the shortfall between employment earnings you will receive and the expenses that you require to maintain a reasonable standard of living.

Rapid economic change

Economic change can be friend or foe depending on how you respond to it. If you are constantly abreast of the changes in your particular industry, occupation, etc., and if you keep your skills and knowledge current and relevant to the marketplace, then change will be your economic friend. If, however, you do not keep abreast of the change and let your knowledge stagnate, then your skills will likely become obsolete and you will have a far greater risk of being unemployed or having a business failure. Therefore, an essential part of your defensive strategy should be to keep informed of actual and pending changes and to do what is necessary to keep on the leading edge of your occupation or business.

Buy/sell agreements

If you are in business with other partners, it is essential that you have a buy/sell agreement that is up to date (i.e., reviewed every year and kept current) and that the agreement be funded. If one of the partners dies, the surviving partners need to have a mechanism by which they can readily sell the shares of the deceased partner for fair market value and immediately receive those funds in cash to benefit the dependents of the deceased partner and to protect themselves.

Many partnerships do not have buy/sell agreements; of those that do, by far the majority do not keep their agreements up to date. Most buy/sell agreements are also inadequately funded, leaving the dependents of the partners in extremely vulnerable positions.

Buy/sell agreements are a vital component of the defensive strategy of every personal financial plan of a business partner or major shareholder of a closely held business. It is essential that your agreement be reviewed regularly and incorporate any changes in government policy. The best way to do this is to have your insurance or tax adviser keep you informed.

Wills and estate planning

Many survivors in families suffer enormous difficulties needlessly because the deceased relative left no will or the will is out of date and cannot do the job. Wills must be reviewed periodically so that overall goals can be accomplished in the event of the death of a family member.

A sound estate plan is simply a financial plan for the disposition after death of your assets (less liabilities and estate expenses) to your beneficiaries. It directs that those assets be used in the most effective way. Tax planning is normally an integral part of this process, as is the determination of insurance requirements (if any) to fund potential tax liabilities on property at death.

Remember, you have a choice: if you do not draw up a will, then the government has one ready for you, whether you and your family like it or not. Have your professional advisers keep you informed of legislative changes in this area as well. (For more information, see *Wills*, another title in the Self-Counsel Series.)

AFTER RETIREMENT: AN OFFENSIVE STRATEGY

When are you going to retire? Estimate this age as accurately as possible and then, if you are a man, anticipate a life expectancy of 81, and if you are a woman, anticipate a life expectancy of 87, unless there are health reasons for projecting otherwise. If your family has a history of longer-than-average life expectancy, taken this into consideration in your planning.

I normally recommend to clients that they divide retirement into two phases for purposes of income and expense projections. The first phase runs from retirement to the mid-seventies and the second phase encompasses the remaining life expectancy. The actual ages can vary depending on anticipated activity levels, health, tax planning, etc. Taking the income requirements that are a reflection of goals in retirement, as well as anticipated pensions and other income, you are ready to calculate the capital required at the beginning of retirement to fund the necessary cost of living throughout life expectancy.

This is a detailed process, as it must take into account all government, company, and private pensions, as well as personal assets and liabilities at retirement.

Assumptions regarding interest rates and inflation are, of course, critical at this stage. Regardless of what inflation and interest rates you choose, historically there has been a 2% to 3% spread (i.e., interest has normally been 2% to 3% higher than inflation). Therefore, whether inflation is 5% and interest rates are 8%, or if interest rates are 10% and inflation is 7%, the real returns are much the same.

Many people underestimate their income requirements in retirement. They assume that because they will probably have their house paid for and will have few monthly expenses, their income requirements will be dramatically reduced. But this is often not the case. In retirement there is a lot more leisure time and, therefore, more time to shop, travel, and, in general, spend money. It is also a time in which people are less inclined to do their own repairs around the house and on their cars, etc., and therefore maintenance costs frequently increase in retirement. Furthermore, the repairs and maintenance required around the house often increase because it is getting older.

An important aspect of an offensive post-retirement strategy is maximizing income through the wise management of pension funds and pension income combined with non-registered capital assets. In Canada, for example, pension income can, with certain limitations, be reinvested in registered savings plans at the present time to age 71 without paying tax on it. (Make sure you keep up to date on the current limits.) Remarkably few people are aware of this. Of those who are, many do not convert their registered savings into pension income until they require the income or at age 71. Consult with your professional adviser for possible legislative changes in the taxation of pension incomes.

Rigorous analysis indicates that whether the income is required or not, it is wise to convert this pension fund into income and reinvest the proceeds into another registered savings plan. Find out if this strategy can work for you.

For most people, particularly those in higher income tax brackets, it is usually a good idea to draw income from non-registered funds by using annuity plans designed for this purpose. This plan can provide a significant tax deferral on interest earnings, resulting in very high after-tax equivalent bond yields. I have seen cases in which the total income tax of a client is reduced by 40% as a result of this program.

The annuity can pay out an income for a guaranteed number of years, or it can pay out an income for life. Again the selection of the term of the annuity will depend on the non-registered capital available and the overall income and expense requirements combined with the pension proceeds that are available.

Pension plans: the most important financial decision of your life

The most important financial decision in many people's lives is the selection of pension options at retirement. Most pension programs, whether they are personal registered programs or company plans, have several options. The first choice is whether the program will be single life or joint life. A joint life program means that payments will be made throughout the lives of the pensioner and spouse for as long as either of them live. Pension payments may be level or indexed.

There is usually an option that the pension payments may be reduced at the death of the pensioner, or it may remain level through to the end of the life of the last survivor. This joint life option may also have a guaranteed period so that if the pensioner and spouse both die, there is a guaranteed number of years of pension payments into the estate.

The single life annuity is for the life of the pensioner only, but also has options for guarantees of 5, 10, 20 years, etc., so that if the pensioner dies, payments will continue to his or her estate for a guaranteed number of years. The joint life annuity varies considerably with the age of the spouse. If the spouse is 10 years younger than the pensioner and female, payments will be considerably reduced compared with a female spouse who is the same age as or older than the pensioner.

There are many variables to consider and pensioners should seek professional help when choosing annuity options. An enlightened decision can only be made in the context of a total personal financial plan.

The pension-option decision is simplified if the pensioner has sufficient permanent insurance in place to look after any dependents exclusive of the pension income. In this case the pensioner can opt for the maximum income, which is the single life option, with a 0-, 5-, or 10-year guarantee. By doing this the pensioner gets maximum benefits while alive. If no permanent insurance is in place, the pensioner will quite often opt for a joint life option, unless he or she has considerable capital assets that can be used by the survivors to generate the necessary income for the balance of their dependencies.

Life planning becomes very important before and during retirement because of the tremendous changes that occur in daily routine and lifestyle. A plan that takes into consideration physical, mental, emotional, and spiritual health is indeed a life and death matter. Statistics show that in the United States executives who have not prepared for retirement receive 13 social security checks on average. In Canada the number is something like 18. They simply do not prepare for the adjustment and die. The retirement years can indeed be the golden years, but some hard thinking and planning must be done to ensure it.

A good offensive life plan and financial plan is one of the best defenses against declining health — physically, mentally, emotionally, spiritually, and financially. In some cases pensioners have no option regarding their pension, particularly if it is a disability pension, and the pension terminates when they do. In such instances, there needs to be sufficient insurance on the pensioner's life to ensure that the survivor is able to carry on with a desired lifestyle.

Emergency funds are required, even more than in the pre-retirement years, due to increased health care needs and repair and maintenance requirements for the residence, etc.

As noted above, a good offensive strategy, well thought out and well prepared, and a well-planned capital accumulation program in the pre-retirement years, will take care of most of the defensive programs required in retirement.

If you are short of the capital needed in retirement to fund the lifestyle you require, it is important that you have a sound financial plan in place throughout your retirement years. Budgeting throughout retirement is a process of rationing your capital so that it does not terminate before you do. Many people who are short of capital in retirement make the mistake of spending all or most of it in the first few years, leaving their remaining years very lean indeed. It is essential to consider interest rates and inflation when rationing out your available capital. It is also critical that you make your capital work as hard for you as possible, which frequently means taking advantage of such instruments as specialized annuity programs. (This is discussed further in Part III.)

Essentially, you will have two options: to spend all of your capital in the first few years of your retirement and then to be left completely dependent on your pension income, or to reduce the expenditure of your capital during the early years of your retirement and ration it out throughout your retirement years.

Most people who spend all of their capital in their initial retirement years, if they had the choice of doing it over again, would much prefer to ration it out throughout their lifetime. (The calculations and budgeting process required to achieve this goal are described in Part III.)

There is also the possibility that you are better off than you think you are, which will make it possible to improve your current standard of living, increase charitable donations if you choose to do so, or take that trip that you always wanted to but never thought you could afford.

PART II
PLANNING FOR LIFE

In this section, we will examine the processes and techniques of financial planning, with the aim of establishing planning strategies suitable to individual lifestyles. The information presented here will enable you to develop your own financial plan in Part III.

A primary theme in this book is that financial plans and goals are meaningless unless they are grounded in a meaningful life plan. It is a theme that bears repetition: if your financial goals are not congruent with your overall life plan, then they will remain little more than idle daydreams and will have little chance of becoming a reality.

LIFE PLANNING AND FINANCIAL PLANNING

Planning for your personal life is not something you learn in school. In school you can learn psychology, business techniques, and ethics, but almost nothing of the practical planning that can help you find fulfillment in your life.

FINANCIAL PLANNING AND YOUR PERSONAL GOALS

Further, outside the world of organized education, there are few places you can turn to for guidance in effective planning. It's not surprising, then, that most people tend to take a piecemeal approach toward life planning and try to prepare for isolated segments of their lives (such as career or retirement), never gaining an integrated approach to life as a whole.

One of the few writers on this subject, Richard Bolles, makes an in-depth study of life planning in his book in *The Three Boxes of Life and How to Get out of Them*. He offers a useful critique of the conventional approach to this important activity, pointing out that most of us try to make our plans by dividing our lives into three boxes: education, work, and retirement. In Bolles' opinion, these neat divisions rarely work. Most people do not simply finish with one part of life and abruptly proceed to the next. By planning for life in this conventional way, many people suffer major injury to their sense of self-worth and purpose when they find themselves, for example, suddenly in retirement with little or no prospect of leading anything other than an idle life and, frequently, with very little money with which to do it.

Bolles approaches the areas of education, work, leisure, and retirement by blending them into a plan that involves a person's whole life, shifting the emphasis from one area to another as age and energy level changes. In this approach, growing old is a real part of a person's plans for being young.

It is just such an integrated approach that I have found to be most useful for me and my clients.

The biggest challenge for financial planners (as well as for other professionals who act as advisers) is to help clients create a future life course that enthuses and motivates them. Most people have trouble with this because their overall life goals remain relatively vague; but effective planning can only be done when the future track becomes very clear and precise.

Because hard thinking, planning, and homework is required to do good life planning and to set meaningful life goals, many people bypass this step in order to get on to the more manageable job of setting out tasks. It may make you feel better to get on to a task that you can manage easily, but overlooking the long run will always mean trouble for you later.

A PLANNING EXERCISE

I use an approach many people have found to be helpful in creating, developing, and clarifying their life goals. This is an exercise, or set of exercises, in imagination. Its purpose is to allow you to participate imaginatively in the future in order to discover your goals today.

First, you must take a little time out and get into a relaxed and positive frame of mind. Listen to your favorite music or go for a walk in the park, or think about the last time that you did something that made you feel good. Do anything that you need to do to help you feel and be very positive in your attitude. After you are in this favorable mind-set, go through the following routine:

(a) Imagine yourself a year from now looking back over the past year. You are very satisfied and very pleased with what has happened.

(b) Picture very clearly the situation that you are in a year from now at work, at home, and in other areas of your life. Picture each scene in detail. See it, hear it in detail, and feel the positiveness in each of these scenes.

(c) Make a written note of what you see, hear, and feel. Note what it is that pleases you so much in each scene. Make the notes sufficiently detailed that you could make a short movie of each scene, complete with dialogue, sound effects, etc. You are the writer, the producer, the director, and the main actor in each of the scenes.

(d) Run these "movies" over in your mind at least three times a day for five minutes, totalling a minimum of fifteen minutes a day. Introduce whatever changes are necessary to make these movies more exciting, more invigorating, more motivating, more self-fulfilling.

(e) Run your "movie" each day for 30 days (minimum 15 minutes a day). The same approach can be used for longer periods of 2 years, 5 years, 10 years, 20 years, etc.

If you are not normally meditative, you may feel a little foolish the first time you try this exercise. But even if you do, stick with it anyway. It's a very healthy kind of meditation, and I personally know it to be a very good way to develop highly motivating life goals. Goals that motivate, enthuse, and compel you to action are emotionally charged, and these five steps, if followed faithfully, will help you take the critical first step toward creating such a motivating set of personal life goals.

Here is an example of the kind of scenario the planning exercise might develop. In this case, a married couple have been thinking about where they will be five years after retirement. Remember, this is where they want to be; it is a reflection of their real desires, not just a fantasy. (All estimates in the example are in 1988 dollars.)

A planning example

> We have been living in Victoria for five years (since retirement). We have a two-bedroom bungalow overlooking the ocean. We have a comfortable car and a motorhome in which we travel to Arizona and New Mexico for the winters. We have traveled abroad every other year for two months at a time.
>
> The bungalow cost $140,000, and our annual housing expense is $2,500 (including taxes, maintenance, fuel, etc.). We have a $10,000 car which we plan on trading in every five years. The motorhome is four years old. We bought it for $27,000 and plan to keep it indefinitely. The annual cost of operating both vehicles is $3,000 (including fuel, repairs, insurance, and an allowance for depreciation). We live in the motorhome for three months of year.
>
> Our food budget is $6,000 a year and our travel budget is $5,000. We like to golf, and spend about $1,000 a year on the golf course. Clothing costs are about $1,500 a year. Our budget for charitable donations, gifts, and miscellaneous items is $2,500 a year.

Once you have developed a comparable scenario suited to your own lifestyle, you will have the information you need to begin working on your own life plan.

It is within the context of a developing sense of your life plan and its goals that we will examine the financial tools and techniques that can make these ambitions a reality in your life. In Part III, we will be looking closely at your own financial plan. By then, you should be working on clarifying your own goals.

PLANNING FOR FUTURE INCOME AND EXPENSES

A good financial program will ensure you an income sufficient to fund the standard of living you want from the present through to the end of your life and provide not only for your own needs, but also for the needs of your dependents (and for planned charitable giving and estate planning, if these are on your priority list). The following graphs demonstrate the basic financial planning principles used to establish the amount of capital you will need to fund a standard of living.

Do not confuse "financial independence" with retirement. The two are not necessarily the same. By financial independence, I mean the point in your life when you reach the financial position where your employment income is no longer required to fund living expenses. Retirement is when you actually stop working.

The capital curve

First, take a look at the capital curve graph. (See Figure #4.) The living expenses line, labeled LE, indicates the money needed this year, next year, and subsequent years to fund an established standard of living. To plot your living expense line, it is necessary to know accurately your daily expenses as well as anticipated travel, education, charitable expenses, etc.

The income line, labeled INC, reflects the income that you can expect to receive (after tax) from now to the end of your life. The sharp drop in the income line occurs at retirement; it represents income from active employment only and does not include income generated by any accumulated capital.

After plotting the income and expense lines, you are then able to estimate the surplus generated during the period before retirement (INC – LE) and the deficit to be expected after retirement (LE – INC). Once you determine the total deficit anticipated in retirement, you can then calculate the capital sum necessary to fund that deficit.

FIGURE #4
THE CAPITAL CURVE
(Income and expenses)

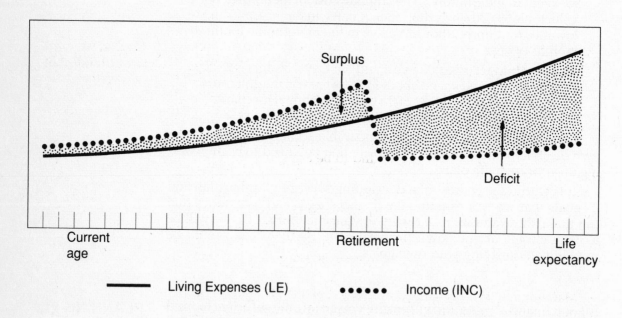

Next, look at the capital curve. (See Figure #5.) The capital accumulation line (CA) represents the capital that must be accumulated during working years to fund the retirement years. Once this capital sum is calculated, the next step is to determine how much capital must be set aside each year to accumulate the required capital before retirement.

The capital curve is the bedrock of your plan. Once you establish an accurate picture of that curve, you can proceed to the tactical work of planning for capital accumulation.

FIGURE #5
THE CAPITAL CURVE
(Capital accumulation)

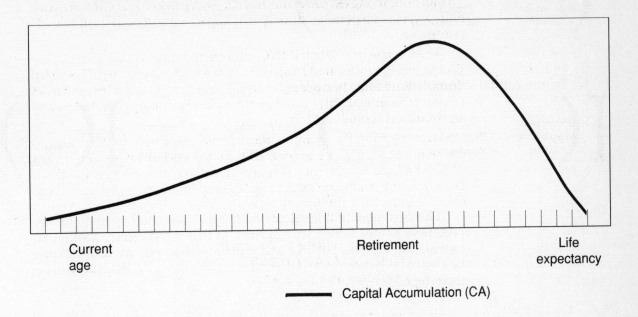

Current age | Retirement | Life expectancy

—— Capital Accumulation (CA)

Generally, capital is accumulated in two ways: in tax-deferred and, for many people, tax-deductible retirement funds such as RRSPs in Canada or IRAs in the United States (which I refer to as registered funds) and in non tax-sheltered funds like term deposits, stocks, real estate, oil and gas, small business ventures, bonds, etc. (which I refer to as non-registered funds). In the United States, there is a third option, the retirement annuity, which allows tax-free accumulation but does not allow the contributions to the fund to be deducted from you income.

You may find, on drawing up these graphs for the first time, that it is impossible to fund your capital accumulation target out of present and future income. If that is the case, it will be necessary to go back to the drawing board and to alter your projected expenses so that they fall within reasonable bounds. (This process is examined in detail in Part III.)

Many of you will prefer perhaps to accept a slightly lower standard of living throughout your entire lifetime rather than suffer a major drop in the last 20 years of your lives.

Conceptually, you are trying to estimate and adjust the following variables:

(a) Current capital accumulation

Capital is accumulated in two ways

(b) Future capital accumulation in current dollars

$$\left(\begin{array}{c} \text{Projected} \\ \text{disposable} \\ \text{income} \end{array} - \begin{array}{c} \text{Projected} \\ \text{expenditures} \end{array} = \begin{array}{c} \text{Projected} \\ \text{surplus} \\ \text{capital for} \\ \text{investment} \\ \text{(or deficit)} \end{array} \right) + \begin{array}{c} \text{Projected} \\ \text{other} \\ \text{capital} \end{array} = \begin{array}{c} \text{Projected} \\ \text{capital} \\ \text{accumulation} \end{array}$$

(c) Future capital accumulation in future dollars

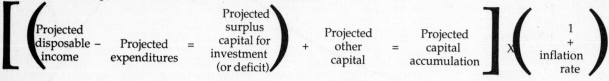

$$\left[\left(\begin{array}{c} \text{Projected} \\ \text{disposable} \\ \text{income} \end{array} - \begin{array}{c} \text{Projected} \\ \text{expenditures} \end{array} = \begin{array}{c} \text{Projected} \\ \text{surplus} \\ \text{capital for} \\ \text{investment} \\ \text{(or deficit)} \end{array} \right) + \begin{array}{c} \text{Projected} \\ \text{other} \\ \text{capital} \end{array} = \begin{array}{c} \text{Projected} \\ \text{capital} \\ \text{accumulation} \end{array} \right] \left(\begin{array}{c} 1 \\ + \\ \text{inflation} \\ \text{rate} \end{array} \right)$$

The third equation is calculated to retirement and again to life expectancy. The variables are adjusted so that the projected capital accumulation remains positive and is not less than zero at the life expectancies of both spouses and provides for any other dependents during their dependency.

Life expectancy

Before you can begin to make your plan, you are the faced with the fundamental question of how long to plan for. This is the key variable and perhaps the most difficult to predict.

Estimating your life expectancy is not as simple as taking the average age of death from the latest census because that kind of statistic can be misleading. In fact, the longer you live, the more likely you are to achieve a greater old age. Most of us underestimate our life expectancy by 5 to 15 years. In fact, a healthy 65-year-old man is well advised to plan on a life expectancy of at least 81 years; a healthy woman of that age should plan for at least 87 years. There are those who maintain that these figures are too optimistic, but I prefer to use them, on the principle that a little left over at the end is preferable to having nothing left before the end. (Appendix 1 contains a life expectancy table.)

Inflation

It is imperative that you take inflation into account when you project future income and expense, as Figure #6 shows. The top line represents cost of living increases if inflation runs at 10% per year, and the bottom line indicates an inflation rate of 5% per year.

Notice that when the cost of living increases at 10% per year, it is necessary for living expenses to double about every 7 years to maintain a constant standard of living. If the inflation rate is only 5%, it is still necessary for a living expense budget to double about every 14 years to maintain a constant standard of living.

Between 1971 and 1984 the cost of living in North America increased over 200%, causing serious problems for people in or near retirement.

The effects of future inflation can be devastating to any financial plan. As most people will live 15 to 20 years into retirement, you must build into your plan enough flexibility to adjust for unforeseen variations in the inflation rate. This can only be done with a plan that can be updated and reviewed at least once a year.

FIGURE #6
EFFECTS OF INFLATION

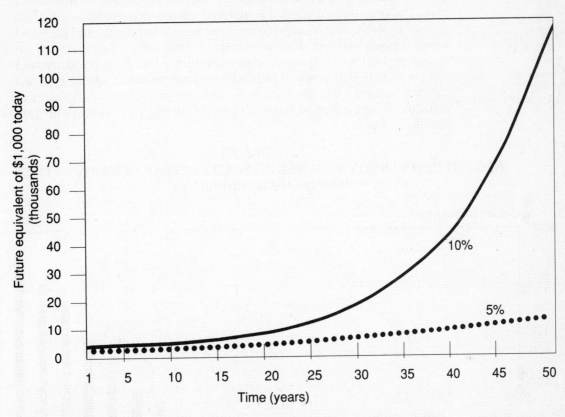

By modifying the capital curve chart previously illustrated (see Figure #4), you can discover the amount of insurance that will be necessary to fund the needs of your dependents (and possibly yourself) in the event of death or disability and loss of income. If you assume the loss of life of a major income earner, you must then reduce your projected income by the appropriate amount. You then determine the capital that is needed to fund that deficit from now throughout the anticipated dependency period. That capital sum (minus personal capital exclusive of residence) will be the amount of insurance you should have in place.

Insurance: life and disability

There may also be other things needing insurance coverage such as debts and liabilities (to creditors and/or to the tax department, for example), which should be retired on the death of the major income earner. The same approach is used to determine the amount of disability insurance you will require.

Disability insurance can be just as important as life insurance; during times of disability not only will income be lost, but frequently expenses will be increased by the treatment of the disability. For those running businesses, insurance is also available to look after business overhead for time during the disability.

ACCUMULATING THE CAPITAL REQUIRED FOR FINANCIAL INDEPENDENCE

Registered funds: RRSPs or IRAs

Everyone, without exception, should be using registered pension plans as a cornerstone of their capital accumulation program. As you can see from the accompanying graphs (see Figures #7 and #8), capital accumulation under a registered plan will grow at a rate two to three times faster than capital outside a registered plan invested in bonds, term deposits, etc. (assuming equal before-tax interest rates and equal growth rates). This results from the special tax status of registered plans: income deposited in a registered plan is not taxed; nor is their annual growth. The income from these registered funds will be taxed when it is withdrawn, of course, but the time value of money and inflation make it much cheaper to pay taxes later rather than sooner; and it is very likely that you will be in a lower tax bracket in retirement than the one you are in today. (Your purchasing power may be greater in retirement than it is now, but with good planning your average tax rate should be lower.)

FIGURE #7
REGISTERED VERSUS NON-REGISTERED CAPITAL ACCUMULATION
(Non-indexed contributions)

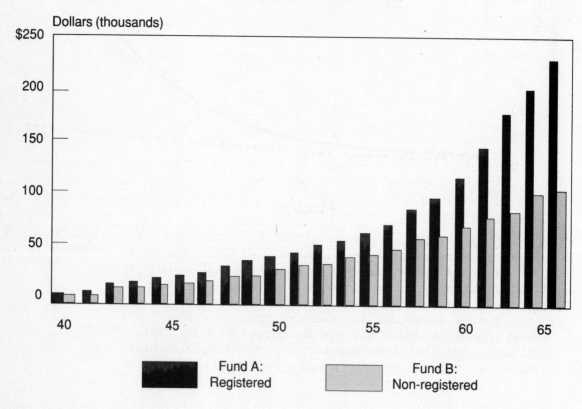

Assumptions: Level contributions

Fund A

1. $2,000 deposited in tax deductible, tax-deferred registered fund at the end of each year from age 40 to 65 (assuming contribution limits not exceeded).
2. 10% return on investment.

Fund B

1. $2,000 gross income less 30% income tax deposited in a savings account (non-registered fund) at the end of each year from age 40 to age 65.
2. 10% return before tax or 7% return after tax (30% marginal tax rate) on non-registered savings.

FIGURE #8
REGISTERED VERSUS NON-REGISTERED CAPITAL ACCUMULATION
(Indexed contributions)

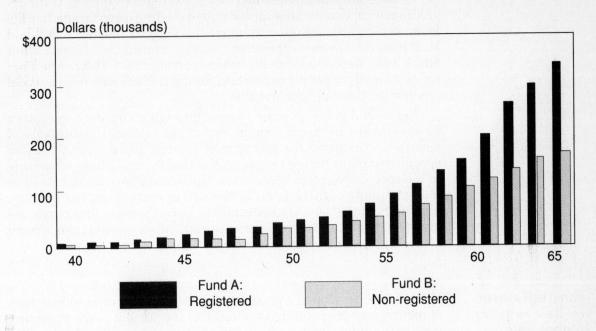

Assumptions: Indexed contributions

Fund A

1. $2,000 indexed at 5% annually deposited in tax deductible, tax-deferred registered fund at the end of each year from age 40 to 65 (assuming contribution limits not exceeded).

2. 10% return on investment

Fund B

1. $2,000 gross income, indexed at 5% annually, less 30% income tax deposited in a savings account (non-registered fund) at the end of each year from age 40 to age 65.

2. 10% return before tax or 7% return after tax (30% marginal tax rate) on non-registered savings.

Registered plans under current legislation can accumulate with no tax until age 71 in Canada and 70.5 in the United States. At that time they must be used to purchase a retirement income, or they can be withdrawn completely, subject to the full payment of income tax at that time. If a retirement income is purchased, the income is taxed as it is received at your then current tax rate.

It is important to note that if the registered plans are in accumulation annuities with the same insurance company that eventually contracts to provide the pension income, there will be a bonus paid with each and every pension check. This can be important over the long run.

Registered plans can be arranged through banks, trust companies, credit unions, life insurance companies, and savings and loan associations. Because the funds accumulated in your registered plans will probably be your largest single asset at retirement, it is very important to know the strength of the company that you are dealing with. Many people will choose the registered savings program that pays the highest rate of interest, but this can mean very little if in the process you lose all or part of your capital because of the company's financial instability.

Often the company that pays the highest rate of interest is not financially strong. You must know who you are doing business with.

Another consideration when looking at registered plans is the degree to which accumulated capital will be creditor-proof. Canadian life insurance companies operate under the Federal Insurance Act and legal precedent demonstrates that funds are more secure from creditor attack when deposited with life insurance companies. This can be a significant factor for people in business for themselves who have a risk of creditor liability or client lawsuits.

Registered plans generate income through guaranteed interest or by investment in stocks, bonds, and other financial instruments. I usually recommend the guaranteed interest plans over the more speculative plans for the simple reason that there is no tax advantage to the speculative plan. Because the registered plans are not taxed as they accumulate, there is no advantage in earning capital gains or dividends in that savings instrument. As well, stocks and bonds are given tax breaks, and are, of course, priced to discriminate against more favorably taxed investment vehicles.

Non-registered funds: regular savings and investment plans

Having first developed a good registered plan, you need to look next at regular non-tax-protected savings and investment plans. For many people, the only effective way to accumulate non-registered funds is to set aside a certain amount of money from each paycheck. A good financial plan will specify how much money must be put aside each month to accumulate the capital needed to meet your personal objectives.

After you have set this money aside, it is important that you determine your own investment profile — that is, establish what kind of an investor you need to be, or want to be. You can entertain higher risk/higher gain possibilities only if you are able to sustain the potential loss. Most of us, of course, are not in a position to afford major capital losses, and, therefore, are limited to relatively conservative savings and investment programs.

At the same time, most people have neither the time nor the expertise (not to mention the dollars needed to diversify sufficiently) to invest in individual equities. Therefore, if you prefer equities, you may want to look at professionally managed funds that are well diversified and are invested only in top quality securities. Again the track record of the company that you are dealing with and the professional managers are critically important.

Many people are surprised to discover that a regular savings program combined with guaranteed interest may be enough to enable them to accomplish their financial objectives over the long run. (Many of my clients, having gone through extensive financial analysis, are relieved to see that their financial objectives can be reached simply by using guaranteed interest rates for their registered as well as non-registered plans.)

The capital gains exemption

Eligible capital gains in Canada are exempt from tax up to a lifetime aggregate of $100,000 per taxpayer. This limit increases to $500,000 for eligible farmers and small businesses. A similar exemption is no longer available in the United States. (See tax manuals for current tax laws on capital gains in both countries.)

What is the most tax efficient, income maximizing strategy for converting your capital into income?

Up to age 70.5 in the United States and 71 in Canada, pension income should usually be spent last rather than first. Many people who have a choice and who do not require their pension incomes bring them into regular income too soon, paying tax needlessly. It is wiser to take non-registered accumulated capital such as stocks, bonds, term deposits, etc. and purchase retirement annuity that minimizes current taxes and maximizes after-tax income.

For example, if you are able to live on the proceeds of a retirement annuity and deposit all pension income in a registered retirement program, the taxes on the non-registered capital are minimized, the current taxes on the pension income are zero, and the accumulated capital under the registered program enjoys maximum growth to age 70.5 or 71. At a 10% interest rate, registered retirement capital will double in under eight years. Make sure that you keep up to date on restrictions on depositing pension income into your registered fund.

If, during those eight years, additional pension income is added to the retirement fund, then the accumulation will be much greater.

In the United States, after-tax capital can be placed in retirement annuities and earn interest without attracting tax. The annuity can then be converted into income after age 59, but before age 70.5. The interest portion of the resulting income is then taxed at your current rate, while the capital portion is not taxed again.

In Canada, tax-free capital growth through interest earnings is not allowed in non-pension funds, but prescribed annuities can be used to defer tax on interest earnings for up to three years prior to first income payment. In my opinion, prescribed annuities are one of the best-kept secrets in retirement income planning in Canada. They are offered by life insurance companies, which are long-term financial institutions, as opposed to banks, which are short-term institutions. Long-range planning involves life insurance and the products of life insurance companies. Banks, on the other hand, can offer good capital accumulation plans through RRSPs and GICs.

Table #2 shows for how many years specific capital amounts will fund specific levels of living expenses, given various inflation and interest rate assumptions.

For example, an amount of $500,000, assuming 6% inflation and 8% interest earnings, and a tax rate of 30%, funding living expenses that are $2,500 per month in current dollars, will last 17 years.

CONVERTING CAPITAL INTO INCOME: WHEN AND HOW

Prescribed annuities: retirement annuities using non-pension funds

Capital required to fund deficits

33

This would be the case for most types of non tax-sheltered investments. If, however, prescribed or retirement annuities are used, the funds will last longer. For an illustration see Table #10 in Part III.

TABLE #2
HOW LONG WILL YOUR MONEY LAST?

CAPITAL SUM	$100,000	$100,000	$250,000	$500,000	$1,000,000	$1,000,000
After-tax income/Mon. (current $)	1,500	1,500	1,500	2,500	2,500	2,500
Marginal tax rate %	30	30	30	30	30	30
Interest %	6	8	6	8	10	8
Inflation %	4	6	4	6	8	6
No. of years until funds are exhausted	5.6	5.5	14.1	16.2	29.1	31.4

PLANNING AND MANAGEMENT

Following is an outline of the five essential phases of any effective and financial planning and implementation process.

As the ancients put it, "For a ship without a port, no wind is the right one."

PHASE 1: Goal development

The most demanding and difficult part of the planning process is, of course, clearly identifying what it is that you really want, and when you want it. To be effective, goals must be highly motivating. They must be something that you really want to achieve, something that you are prepared to make sacrifices for. We all have choices before us; unless we have goals that strongly motivate us, our choices will be inconsistent, frequently contradictory, and, over the long run, will not accomplish a foreseeable outcome.

Goals should be established for one-year, five-year, ten-year, twenty-year, and lifetime intervals.

Start with the goal development process described in the Planning Exercise (see page 24). Go through the exercise focusing on your situation as it will be one year from now. Then repeat it for your situation two and then five years from now; and then for each five-year interval up to your projected age at financial independence.

When you go through it the first time look at the very broad total life picture. Then go through it the second time paying more attention to the things you want to do and the things you want to buy and the planned charitable giving you want to do at the intervals suggested above. How much will you need to buy the food, clothing, shelter, travel, and education you want for you and your dependents?

The next step is to be specific about food, clothing, shelter, education, travel, leisure activities, charitable activities, etc., and then to define the cost of the standard of living you have targeted at different points in the future.

We might call this process the "expense meditation." Follow that with an "income meditation." Picture, hear, and feel what you will be doing in the future, and the kinds of incomes that you will be generating, and then make income projections accordingly. These exercises, of course, need to be tempered somewhat by current income, expenses, assets, and liabilities, particularly in the short term. But as the time frame extends past one year, these longer range "goals" can become more detached from the present situation.

At this stage, do your estimating in present-day dollars. You can factor in the inflation later on.

The planning process, be it personal or corporate, will always tend to dissolve if this stage of the process is neglected. Go right back to very basic values and beliefs. What is it that is important to you? What is it that really matters in your life over the long run? A quiet retreat and some time for meaningful reflection, as well as some good reading to help you get a clearer focus on the meaning and desired direction of your life will help at this phase of your planning process. Take some time with the planning exercise and consider some of the reference readings cited at the end of the book. It will pay big dividends not only in terms of achieving the desired standard of living that you want throughout your lifetime, but it also could be a very significant, enlivening spiritual experience for you.

After this rather abstract process, it is necessary to go into detail, specifying down to the dollar income, expense, and goals for each time frame you are planning. Only by having very specific targets will you be able to measure the degree to which you are on or off target as you implement your plan.

Now, what about post-retirement? Take yourself through the same process, thinking about your post-retirement years. What will you be doing for the first five years of your financial independence? Then focus on 10 years, and so on, through your entire life expectancy. Where do you want to live? How much do you want to travel? What do you want to do during each period of time?

Talk with people who are in retirement now, at the stage of financial independence. Find out from them what their experience has been compared with what they thought it would be. Ask them to compare what they are doing today with what they had anticipated they would be doing.

PHASE 2: Evaluating your present circumstances

To develop your personal financial plan, you have to analyze your income and expense picture. Employee benefits, pension programs, disability, life and general insurance programs are all part of this picture. This will be accompanied with an inventory of assets and liabilities.

You may have to go back over the last year and review your checkbook records in detail. Items like food, clothing, housing, education, travel, leisure activities, charitable giving, gifts, insurance, etc., are a few of the many things that must be accounted for in detail. All sources of income must be accounted for as well.

Calculating your present after-tax income can be achieved simply by referring to your last year's tax return. You also need to evaluate your current assets and liabilities. (The worksheets in Part III will enable you to do these calculations.)

Net worth

Once you know your assets and liabilities you will be able to estimate your net worth.

When you determine the capital accumulation required for financial independence, subtract the value of your personal residence and personal property from your net worth to determine capital available for the generation of income if necessary in the future. If you have some investments that are locked in and are not available to earn current rates of interest or capital appreciation, then these should be noted as well. All of this information is necessary at the planning stage. (Part III contains forms for summarizing income and expenses, assets and liabilities.)

Trends

It is also important to note trends. Is your income increasing or decreasing? Are increases or decreases due to one-time-only gifts? Have there been major one-time expenses incurred as well? These kinds of things should not be allowed to distort a trend analysis. Trends in assets and liabilities are also significant. This kind of analysis will tell you where you will be in the future if you continue on a present course.

PHASE 3: Strategies

Your offensive strategy is the method by which you will achieve your goal. Offensive tactics provide the step-by-step means to generate and maximize income. They also provide step-by-step budget plans. Effective tax planning is a part of good offensive planning.

Your defensive strategy is the method by which you will protect yourself when your assumptions of good health, normal life expectancy, and reasonable economic environment do not turn out as anticipated. Defensive tactics make provision for insurance and emergency funds, as well as contingency plans to augment the family income and reduce living expenses if required. It is better to have defensive strategies in place before an emergency than to have to hastily formulate a strategy in the midst of an emergency. Disasters are what happen when you are not prepared for them.

These strategies can be conveniently divided into pre-financial independence and post-financial independence phases.

The strategic phase of your plan involves looking at the possible ways of moving beyond the first step within specific time frames. After a preliminary look at the possible alternatives, you can then begin to narrow them down to the two or three that, on the surface, appear to be most effective and efficient. This can require a lot of calculation (or reference to tables that are based on extensive calculations). At this stage, begin to build in inflation assumptions and interest rate factors.

Your strategy must, of course, take into account life expectancy. The variables and assumptions you have to work into your projections are at best "guesstimates," and the following factors will have to be reviewed annually: interest rates, inflation, number of years to retirement, income levels, and longevity. Even if the eventual outcome of your plan 20 years from now is very different from what you presently project, by making modifications and corrections each year, you should be able to avoid having to introduce any major changes to your program in any one year.

This step will require detailed cash flow projections — as detailed as you can make them. Relatively close projections can be made for the cost of food, clothing, shelter, and education, as well as income from employment. Depending on your age and marital and family status, you will want to include such things as travel and education for the children or for yourself, charitable giving, a new home, boat, etc. These need to be estimated and scheduled as accurately as possible.

Gifts, if they can be anticipated, or a sale of capital gains earning assets should be planned for as well. By then you will be ready to complete income and expense projections throughout your entire life expectancy. (A life expectancy table is included in Appendix 1.)

A computer can be of great assistance at the detailed stage of the planning process, allowing you to fairly easily consider a variety of scenarios, narrowing down alternatives to two or three options very quickly and accurately. (I do over eight million calculations with my computer when processing even simple retirement income and expense plans.) But if you are not already familiar with computers, the time spent learning may not be the best investment you can make. The worksheets in this book are designed to allow you to make projections yourself. All of the preliminary work — setting goals, assessing your current position, and establishing income and expense projections, for instance — must be done regardless of whether a computer might be needed to make your forecasts. At that stage, you might consider going to a professional planner for assistance.

PHASE 4: Putting the plan into action

Having reached the stage of going into action, you will probably want to involve the help of a number of professionals: a financial planner, lawyer, accountant, insurance agent, stock broker, realtor, etc. With a comprehensive financial plan in hand, you will be in a position to instruct professional advisers in a meaningful way. It is their job, within their fields of expertise, to help you accomplish goals that only you can set. Without a plan, and without this kind of direction, professional advisers have no way of knowing whether or not their collective efforts are congruent or contradictory. Any good professional will be pleased to follow your directions when your objectives are clear and concise.

Savings and investments

A major decision at this stage is the disposition of your savings and investments. Where are you going to put your money, and for how long?

Before you can do this, you (and your investment adviser) must understand your investment profile in depth. Your savings and investment program must match your investment profile as well as be targeted on your planning goals. It is only after you have examined in depth your income, expenses, assets, and liabilities, that you will be able to determine whether or not you are still at the level of providing for your basic needs from now throughout your lifetime, or whether you might be past that and in a position to take higher risks if you wish.

Commitment and motivation are the key to successfully enacting your plans. If you are not committed to or motivated by your goals — financial or other — then you will probably procrastinate and never implement your plan. If, however, you have developed appropriate goals and formulated a good plan, implementation will be a very natural and easy step.

PHASE 5:
Review the plan

Social, economic, and political change can make the best plan obsolete. Regular review and periodic adjustment are vitally important to the success of any strategic plan. Your goals and priorities will also change over time, and your strategy should change with them. Birth and death, marriage, divorce, and aging are all part of the great cycle of change. Changes in tax and estate laws, economic cycles, longevity, new financial instruments entering the marketplace daily, interest rates, and changing government policy and pension programs can all be significant in your personal financial affairs.

A major breakthrough in heart disease and cancer research, for example, could have a dramatic effect on life expectancy. The consequences of this potential change in longevity will be much greater than anyone can anticipate.

Therefore, it will be necessary not only to put your plan into action, but to periodically review and adjust it. Regular reviews of projected versus actual income and expenses are essential if you are going to stay on track. A certain degree of self-discipline can go a long way to helping you achieve your objectives. There are always many persuaders whose job it is to get you off your track and onto theirs. And so I emphasize again the importance of the first step in planning: setting out those goals. They've got to be real for you.

Even as your long-range goals change throughout your lifetime and interest rates and inflation fluctuate, you can make those small annual modifications in your planning tactics that can result in major alterations to your plan over the long run.

Each year will give you that much more experience as a planner, and you will find that you and your "financial team" will become more effective and more efficient as time goes on.

THE FINANCIAL TOOLS FOR CAPITAL ACCUMULATION

Calculating the capital required for financial independence

Preparing for financial independence is the process of accumulating capital to eventually convert it to income to pay for living expenses (including taxes) after employment income ceases or falls to less than expenses. Here is a brief summary of the process:

(a) Project living expenses from now to retirement.

(b) Consider changes in lifestyle (if any) that will occur in retirement, including residence, travel, additional leisure time, etc. Then project annual living expenses throughout retirement.

(c) Project pension and other income in retirement, including any government assistance.

(d) Find the surplus or shortfall between income and expenses.

(e) If expenses exceed income, then calculate the capital required at retirement to generate the required income to meet these unfunded living expenses.

(f) Estimate investment capital available at retirement. If this amount is equal to or exceeds the capital required in (e), then your retirement income will be adequately funded if your projected capital does, in fact, materialize.

(g) If projected available capital is less than required capital, then design an annual savings program to begin immediately to provide the necessary capital. (Alternatively, your retirement standard of living can be reduced accordingly.)

HOW MUCH CAPITAL DO YOU NEED?

Tables #3 and #4 and Figures #9, #10, and #11 following illustrate the amount of income for living expenses that can be generated under varying assumptions, as follows:

(a) Annual interest rate: 6%

(b) Annual inflation rate: 4%.

(c) Annual deposit/index rate: $2,000/year @ 5%

(d) Average tax rate: 30%.

(e) Current age: 40, 45, 50, 55

(f) Retirement age: 60, 65, 70

(g) Life expectancy: 87

Here's an example of how to use these tables. Consider a man who is 40, wishes to retire at 65, and estimates a pre-tax requirement of $12,000 (current dollars) per year until age 87. To accomplish this, he will need to save approximately $6,264 of registered funds per year, indexed at 4%. This number is calculated by looking up the appropriate "current age" and "retire at age" columns, then using the 0.522 factor in the last column, multiplying it by the desired pre-tax income required for living expenses to obtain the annual savings figure of $6,264. Figure #11 illustrates the pattern of growth and depletion this particular accumulation fund would follow.

MAXIMIZE CAPITAL ACCUMULATION USING REGISTERED FUNDS

Your first choice for the investment of surplus income (beyond living expenses) will be savings in the form of registered funds. The reason is simple: money invested in these programs is deducted from income tax; the annual accumulation is not taxed either. The contributions and the income earned on them are only taxed when taken into personal income.

Registered savings grow at two to three times the rate of non-registered savings (depending on your marginal tax rate). Look again at Figures #7 and #8.

TABLE #3
CAPITAL ACCUMULATION USING REGISTERED MONEY
TO GENERATE AN INCOME THAT WILL MEET
UNFUNDED LIVING EXPENSES DURING RETIREMENT

Current age	Retire at age	Initial registered deposit*	Annual income generated**	$1 savings generates an income of***	$1 of income requires savings of****
40	60	2,000	2,440	1.220	0.820
40	65	2,000	3,830	1.915	0.522
40	70	2,000	6,030	3.015	0.332
45	60	2,000	1,700	0.850	1.176
45	65	2,000	2,850	1.425	0.702
45	70	2,000	4,680	2.340	0.427
50	60	2,000	1,050	0.525	1.905
50	65	2,000	1,980	0.990	1.010
50	70	2,000	3,480	1.740	0.575
55	60	2,000	490	0.245	4.082
55	65	2,000	1,230	0.615	1.626
55	70	2,000	2,430	1.215	0.823

* $2,000 annual ($166.67/month) deposit of registered funds, indexed at 5% and accumulated at 6% interest from current age until retirement.

** $2,000 of annual registered savings, indexed at 5% and accumulated at 6% interest from current age until retirement, will generate this pre-tax current dollar income from retirement until age 87.

*** $1 of annual registered savings, indexed at 5% and accumulated at 6% interest from current age until retirement, will generate this pre-tax current dollar income from retirement age until age 87.

**** $1 of annual, pre-tax current dollar income, from retirement until age 87, requires this annual registered savings, indexed at 5% and accumulated at 6% interest from current age until retirement.

TABLE #4
CAPITAL ACCUMULATION USING NON-REGISTERED MONEY
TO GENERATE AN INCOME THAT WILL MEET
UNFUNDED LIVING EXPENSES DURING RETIREMENT

Current age	Retire at age	Initial non-registered deposit*	Annual income generated**	$1 savings generates an income of***	$1 of income requires savings of****
40	60	2,000	1,650	0.825	1.212
40	65	2,000	2,550	1.275	0.784
40	70	2,000	4,010	2.005	0.499
45	60	2,000	1,190	0.595	1.681
45	65	2,000	1,980	0.990	1.010
45	70	2,000	3,250	1.625	0.615
50	60	2,000	770	0.385	2.597
50	65	2,000	1,440	0.720	1.389
50	70	2,000	2,520	1.260	0.794
55	60	2,000	370	0.185	5.405
55	65	2,000	930	0.465	2.151
55	70	2,000	1,830	0.915	1.093

* $2,000 annual ($166.67/month) deposit of non-registered funds, indexed at 5% and accumulated at 6% interest (4.2% after tax) from current age until retirement.

** $2,000 of annual non-registered savings, indexed at 5% and accumulated at 6% interest (4.2% after tax) from current age until retirement, will generate this after-tax current dollar income from retirement until age 87.

*** $1 of annual non-registered savings, indexed at 5% and accumulated at 6% interest (4.2% after tax) from current age until retirement, will generate this after-tax current dollar income from retirement age until age 87.

**** $1 of annual, after-tax current dollar income, from retirement until age 87, requires this annual non-registered savings, indexed at 5% and accumulated at 6% interest (4.2%) from current age until retirement.

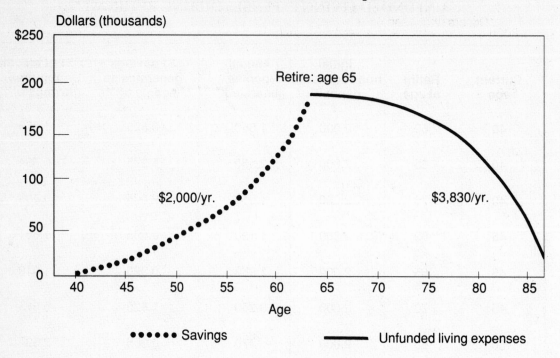

FIGURE #9
RETIREMENT CAPITAL: REGISTERED SAVINGS
(Fund accumulation and depletion)

Dollars (thousands)

Retire: age 65

$2,000/yr.

$3,830/yr.

Age

•••••• Savings   —— Unfunded living expenses

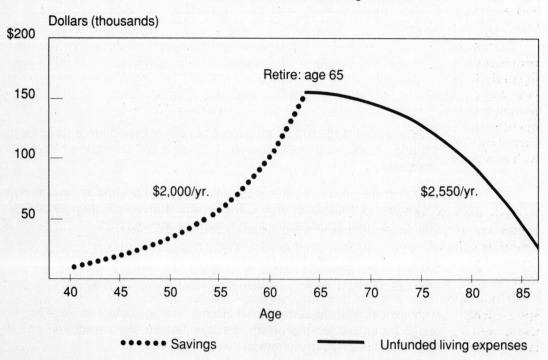

FIGURE #10
RETIREMENT CAPITAL: NON-REGISTERED SAVINGS
(Fund accumulation and depletion)

Dollars (thousands)

Retire: age 65

$2,000/yr.

$2,550/yr.

Age

•••••• Savings   —— Unfunded living expenses

42

FIGURE #11
RETIREMENT CAPITAL: REGISTERED SAVINGS
(Fund accumulation and depletion)

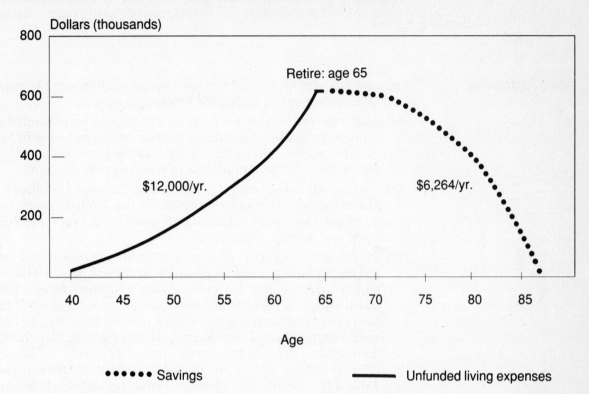

Dollars (thousands)

Retire: age 65

$12,000/yr.

$6,264/yr.

Age

●●●●● Savings   —— Unfunded living expenses

Non-registered funds: tax shelters

From time to time the government encourages investment in specific sectors of the economy by providing tax shelter incentives. If the investments are sound and if the sponsoring companies have integrity and a good track record, then these opportunities can be excellent vehicles for capital accumulation.

But tax shelter schemes should be approached with caution. Many people investing in tax shelters do so with little or no prior analysis of the underlying strength of the investment or the company involved. If you are considering tax shelters, make sure that you do your homework. Many investors have lost all of their equity and have frequently and unwittingly found themselves liable for other debts incurred by the tax shelter, sometimes costing an entire life's savings, as well as a claim on future income.

Spousal incomes

Arrange your registered and non-registered funds so that spousal incomes are as close to equal as possible during retirement. An appropriate spousal income arrangement is an important factor to your financial planning, but many people fail to appreciate it until it is too late.

If one spouse is not earning eligible employment income, the spouse who is earning the eligible income should, as much as possible, use spousal registered plans to equalize the registered capital accumulated in the names of both spouses. In retirement the income will be attributed to the spouse in whose name the pension plan is registered, so be sure both names are there. This can make a considerable difference in the total amount of tax paid by a couple.

It is also important that non-registered funds, as much as possible, are accumulated in the names of both spouses during accumulation years.

After retirement   The accumulation of registered and non-registered funds can be maximized after retirement by taking the following steps:

(a) Maximize rollovers of the pension income that is not needed to fund living expenses into accumulation funds, up to age 70.5 or 71. This serves to minimize your **taxable** income, and maximizes the capital accumulation in your pension program.

(b) Use tax-advantage programs such as retirement annuities for accumulating non-pension capital in the United States and prescribed annuities in Canada for generating a retirement income and deferring taxable income.

(c) Purchase the best benefit-to-cost ratio life insurance that will last throughout your life expectancy. Sufficient personal life insurance at retirement can increase your retirement income substantially if you select single life income options instead of the lower joint life income options. For example, the difference between single life and joint life annuities for a male, depending on his wife's age, can frequently average 10% to 20%. This difference can be significant throughout your retirement (see Table #1). The difference between joint life and single life annuities is the cost of insurance. With permanent cost effective insurance in place on your life, you will be able to opt for the higher income from a single life annuity.

Through the proper choice of life insurance, you are able to enjoy a higher standard of living during your retirement. If you are able to save some of your pension income, the additional single life pension income will accumulate significantly faster than the joint life income. (And remember your pension income can be accumulated **tax free,** up to age 70.5 in the United States and 71 in Canada.) Again, check with your advisers on this point.

If your pension income is 20% greater because you have purchased permanent insurance separate and apart from the annuity contract, then you will be able to maximize your capital accumulation — especially during the early years of your retirement when you will not require all your registered and non-registered retirement income.

Another advantage of private insurance enabling the selection of the higher income single life option is flexibility. If the spouse (who is the second life of the joint annuity) departs due to death or other causes, the annuitant can discontinue the insurance, take the cash values, and continue to receive the maximum pension income.

A good financial plan will ensure that you do not use all your income in early retirement years in order to combat inflation in later years.

Review the three points above until you thoroughly understand them. Discuss them with your adviser if need be. These points are frequently misunderstood.

I always recommend to my clients that they make their registered retirement and pension investments very conservatively and that their non-registered investments, at least up to the point required to fund a minimum acceptable standard of living, be very conservative as well. Only after they have covered the essentials, and if there is non-registered capital available for investment above and beyond the essential capital required to fund emergencies and post-retirement expenditures, should they even consider higher risk investments.

If taking risks is part of your business, then it is important that you set aside 10% to 15% of your profits annually and place them in creditor-proof, blue-chip, or guaranteed-interest programs. If you need convincing arguments, talk to those who didn't and now wish they had. They're not hard to find.

Worksheet #1, below, is designed to help you determine your profile as an investor and decide what kind of investments are most appropriate for you. The worksheet can be applied to your total holdings or to your next investment only.

Worksheet #2, the savings/investment checklist, can then be used to determine how consistent your individual assets are with your investment preferences.

A lot of people lose a lot of money in high-risk ventures they assumed they could never lose. These people forget the simple fact that increasing risk increases the probability of loss. Remember: there is never a potentially high return unless there is a high risk to go along with it.

WORKSHEET #1
INVESTOR PROFILE

Investment Characteristic	Importance					
	0 (Low)	1	2	3	4	5 (High)
Risk						
Return						
Liquidity						
Cash flow						
Term						
Inflation protection						
Tax benefits						
Mangagement effort						

WORKSHEET #2
SAVINGS/INVESTMENT CHECKLIST
(Consistent with investment preferences?)

Asset	Risk		Return		Liquidity		Cash flow		Term		Inflation protection		Tax benefits		Management effort	
	Yes	No	Yes	No	Yes	No	Yes	No	Yes	No	Yes	No	Yes	No	Yes	No

In the event of accident, sickness, or death, income insurance plans are available in two general forms:

(a) lump sum payments

(b) regular payments (monthly or annual)

Disability income can be taxable or non-taxable. If disability income insurance is purchased by the individual, the proceeds are tax-free. If the disability income insurance is purchased by a company, however, the proceeds are taxable. A good rule of thumb is to purchase disability income insurance that is indexed, tax free, and equal to two-thirds of your current earned income before tax.

Some insurance companies have a 15-day cancellation period on group insurance; that is, if they decide that they no longer want to continue the insurance contract, they can give a 15-day notice to cancel. For most people, this kind of insurance is inappropriate for the long term, and they will consider private coverage to ensure that the insurance will be in place when they need it and that possible changes in personal health will not preclude them from purchasing coverage when they need it.

"Own-occupation" disability income insurance pays benefits if you are unable to continue to work at your specific occupation. "Any-occupation" disability income insurance only pays benefits if you are unable to work at all. As you can see, there is a considerable difference in the two types of coverage.

Before purchasing a plan that pays out a lump sum after a specified waiting period, you need to know how big that lump sum should be. It should be big enough to fund your living expenses as calculated in Worksheet #10 on page 77. (The section on life insurance in Part III addresses this question in more detail.)

There are other considerations to take into account. For how many months or years will the payments come in? How long is the waiting period after the disability until the payments start? Is the size of the payment affected by your other income, or is it fixed? What is the insurer's exact definition of disability? These and many other questions suggest that you get competent professional help in this area. You need a disability income insurance plan that fits your overall goals.

Let's assume that you die unexpectedly tomorrow leaving your dependents to fend for themselves. How much capital will they need to maintain their standard of living? (Be sure to take inflation into account.)

First, project the living expenses of your dependents. Second, estimate all anticipated income sources for these dependents. Third, calculate the deficit, if any, that is equal to the unfunded annual living expenses. Finally, calculate the capital needed to generate the required after-tax income.

You need to estimate several figures at this point:

(a) Your anticipated interest, dividend, and capital gains earnings on capital

(b) Your personal average income tax rate

(c) Your life expectancy (See Appendix 1.)

(d) Whether government assistance such as the Canada Pension/Social Security will be available or significant when you become an eligible recipient

(e) What the inflation rate will be

(f) What other investment capital will exist at death (i.e., How much after-tax investment capital will be available at the time of income earner's death?)

Given the above data, you can compute the capital required to fund your dependents' unfunded living expenses net of all government-income assistance or existing sources of person income.

Some typical cases

The graphs and Table #5 following illustrate capital requirements for several typical cases of persons from ages 30 to 70. The assumptions are as follows:

(a) Annual interest rate: 6%

(b) Inflation: 4%

(c) Average tax rate: 30%

(d) Surviving spouse's life expectancy: 87

(e) $10,000 (in current dollars) after tax is amount required to meet unfunded living expenses.

Figures #12 to #20 illustrate insurance capital required to provide an after-tax income of $10,000 per year (in current dollars) to fund living expenses.

FIGURE #12
INSURANCE CAPITAL REQUIREMENTS
(Age 30)

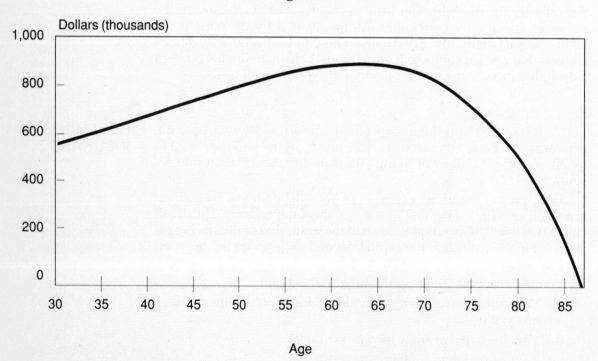

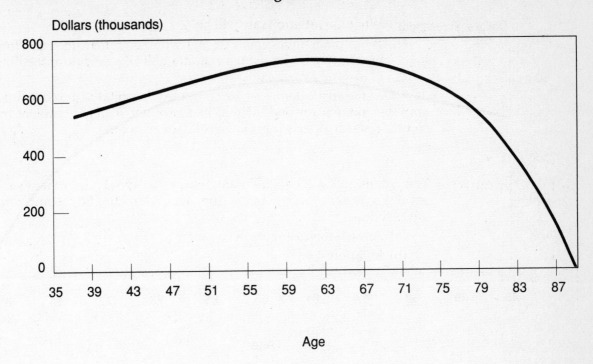

FIGURE #13
INSURANCE CAPITAL REQUIREMENTS
(Age 35)

Dollars (thousands)

Age

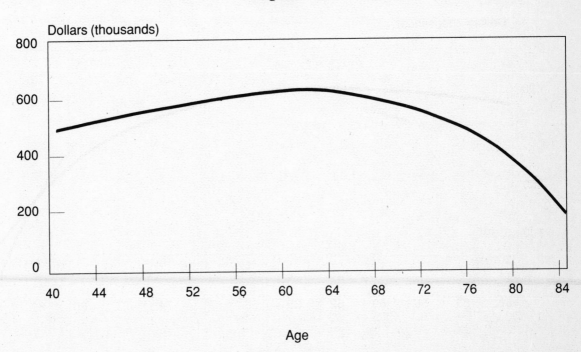

FIGURE #14
INSURANCE CAPITAL REQUIREMENTS
(Age 40)

Dollars (thousands)

Age

FIGURE #15
INSURANCE CAPITAL REQUIREMENTS
(Age 45)

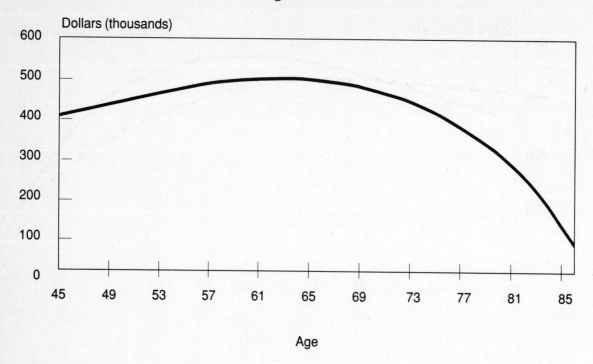

Dollars (thousands)

Age

FIGURE #16
INSURANCE CAPITAL REQUIREMENTS
(Age 50)

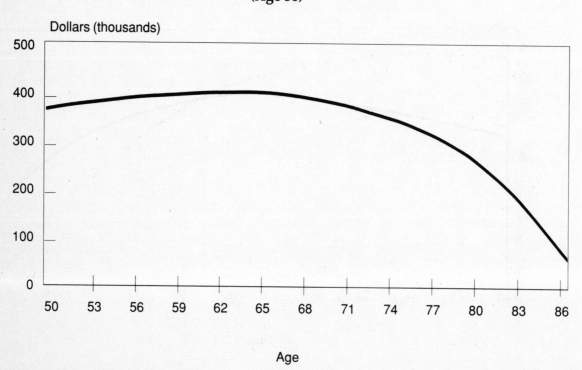

Dollars (thousands)

Age

FIGURE #17
INSURANCE CAPITAL REQUIREMENTS
(Age 55)

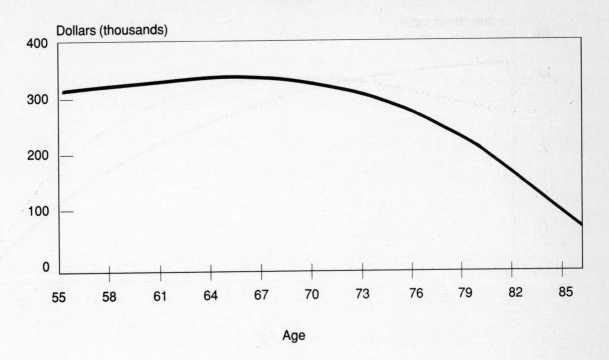

Dollars (thousands)

Age

FIGURE #18
INSURANCE CAPITAL REQUIREMENTS
(Age 60)

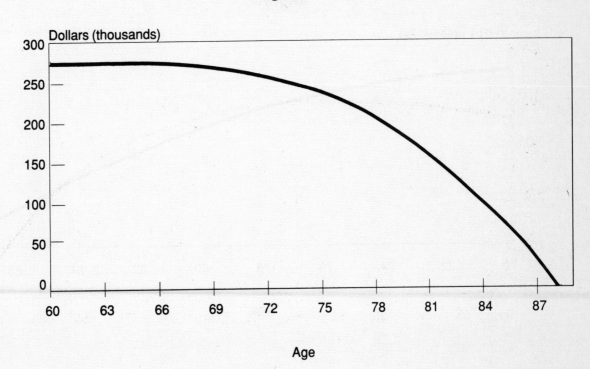

Dollars (thousands)

Age

FIGURE #19
INSURANCE CAPITAL REQUIREMENTS
(Age 65)

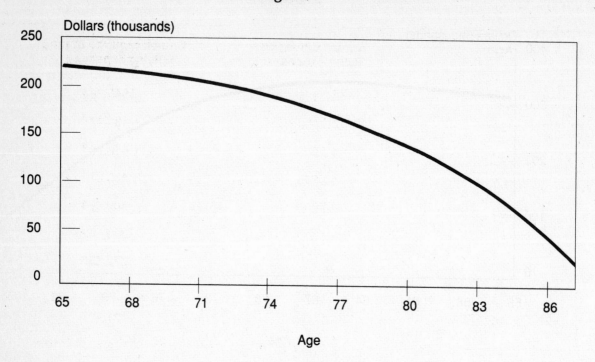

Dollars (thousands)

Age

FIGURE #20
INSURANCE CAPITAL REQUIREMENTS
(Age 70)

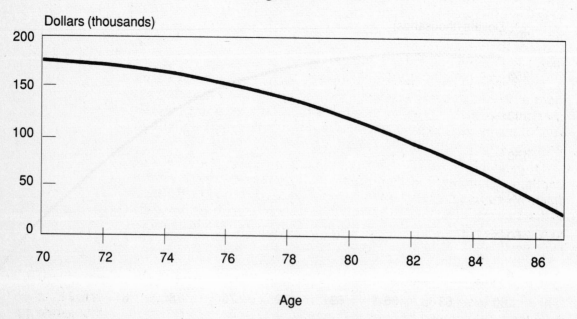

Dollars (thousands)

Age

52

TABLE #5
LIFE INSURANCE REQUIRED TO FUND
SURVIVORS' ANNUAL EXPENDITURES

Age	Annual unfunded living expenses	Capital required to fund living expenses
30	$10,000	$549,386
35	10,000	504,477
40	10,000	458,987
45	10,000	413,213
50	10,000	366,889
55	10,000	320,242
60	10,000	272,936
65	10,000	225,336
70	10,000	177,107

These graphs illustrate how the capital fund grows during the first few years, and then begins to decline rapidly due to the effects of taxes and inflation.

Look at the graph for age 40 (see Figure #14). Based on the above assumptions, 40-year-old individuals who die, become totally disabled, or otherwise lose all alternative sources of income today, will require $458,987 of capital now to fund their own living expenses and/or those of their dependents at the annual rate of $10,000 (in current dollars).

From age 40 to 63, the annual growth of the fund exceeds the annual increases in living expenses and the capital grows steadily to a maximum of $602,229 at age 63. From 64 to 87 the living expenses exceed the annual growth of the fund and the capital depletes with increasing speed until it is all used up at age 87.

If available personal after-tax investment capital is less than the capital required to fund dependents' living expenses, the shortfall is normally funded by life insurance. The unique advantage of insurance is that the very event that triggers the need for capital (death of income earner) causes the capital to be paid immediately to the dependents who need it.

What kind of insurance do you need?

The first question you should ask before taking out any insurance is how long do you need it? This will be enough to make the fundamental choice between term and permanent.

If the answer is less than five years, then term insurance will be the most cost effective. If the answer is more than five years (or definitely more than ten), permanent insurance becomes the best buy for most people. Cash flow restriction may prevent some people from buying the permanent insurance, but wherever possible it should be the insurance of choice for the longer term.

Term versus permanent

The term-versus-permanent argument has been a favorite among consumer advocates who invariably favor the apparently cheaper and "purer" term insurance. But the argument is misleading. A rigorous financial analysis that considers the time value of money will demonstrate the inherent weakness in buying short-term insurance for extended periods of time. (See Table #6.)

TABLE #6
NET COST TERM VERSUS PERMANENT INSURANCE
PREPARED FOR MALE NON-SMOKER AGE 30*

$100,000 Permanent Insurance

Year	Total premiums paid	Total cash value	Net gain cash value minus premium	Net gain death benefit minus premium
1	$461	$45	($416)	$99,539
5	2,307	55	(2,252)	97,693
10	4,615	3,001	(1,614)	95,385
15	6,922	6,614	(308)	(3,078)
20	8,768	10,745	1,977	91,232
Age 60	8,768	20,021	11.253	91,232
Age 65	8,768	27,110	18,342	91,232
Age 70	8,768	35,364	26,596	91,232

$100,000 Five-Year Renewable and Convertible Term Insurance

Year	Total premium paid	Total cash value	Net gain cash value minus premium	Net gain death benefit minus premium
1	$155	0	($155)	$99,845
5	775	0	(755)	99,225
10	1,635	0	(1,635)	98,365
15	2,730	0	(2,730)	97,270
20	4,335	0	(4,335)	95,665
Age 60	10,105	0	(10,105)	89,895
Age 65	15,350	0	(15,350)	84,650
Age 70	24,040	0	(24,040)	75,960

* The time value of money is not considered in this illustration.

In Table #6, a 30 year-old male non-smoker is deciding between $100,000 of permanent insurance and $100,000 of term insurance, given the rates currently in effect for a large insurance company.

In this case, the term insurance premiums increase every five years and are fixed. The permanent annual premium is also fixed but the company's estimate of future dividends is not. If the assumed dividend scale is realized, then under the premium offset provision the annual dividends will be applied to cover all of the premium payments after 19 years. If the policies are held for 10 years or more and are then surrendered, the permanent insurance proves to be more economical because the net gain of expected cash surrender value less accumulated premiums is higher than it is for term insurance. For example, if the policies are surrendered at age 70, the net savings from purchasing permanent rather than term insurance will be $50,636, assuming that the expected dividend scale on the permanent insurance is realized.

If the insured survives for more than about 25 years (and it is very likely that he will) and then dies, the permanent is again more economical because the net gain of the death benefit less accumulated premiums is higher than it is for term insurance.

For example, if the insured dies at age 70, the net gain from purchasing permanent rather than term insurance can be estimated at $15,272 ($91,232 - $75,960), assuming that the permanent expected dividend scale is realized. Further, since term insurance premiums become so expensive in later years, most holders eventually cancel, take a lower pension income (by using joint life annuities rather than single life annuities protected by the insurance), and their dependents receive no insurance death benefit. Less than 2% of all term insurance contracts ever pay out death benefits, since term insurance is almost always out of force at death.

Another important factor in considering term versus permanent insurance is the probability of an adverse economic situation rendering you unable to keep up the premiums. If this is a possibility, then the case is very strong for a permanent insurance product that will fund its own premium during such times. Many people assume that they can drop insurance and then be insured again at some time in the future. But the times of economic adversity are the times when insurance is needed most, and you may not be able to qualify for the insurance that is required at the later time for health reasons.

Variable premiums and risk

If you are considering permanent insurance directly linked to interest-sensitive money market instruments or directly tied to equity funds, you should know the downside as well as the upside of such a contract.

Remember that if the interest rate falls or if the value of the securities to which your insurance is directly linked drops, you will incur an increase in premium or your insurance coverage will decrease. (Conversely, of course, rising interest rates or security values will work to your benefit.) This kind of insurance ties in a speculative factor and, therefore, a risk factor that you may not be able to afford.

Second, do you think that the upside potential of a variable premium product outweighs the downside potential (assuming that you can afford the downside)? If your answer is yes in each case, you have an argument in favor of the variable premium product.

(**Note:** Many products such as those tied to equities and/or interest rates will vary the premium and/or the amount of insurance.)

Once you know how much insurance you need, plan to keep that amount in place. If your insurance is a variable premium product be sure that you will always be able to afford the higher premiums if they go up. If you can't be sure, then don't buy variable-premium insurance. (See Table #7.)

Don't take risks that you can't afford. Insurance contracts are for the long term. All other things being equal, deal only with the financially strongest and best-managed companies in the business. Weaker companies always have to offer a little better deal simply to stay in business. You have to decide whether or not you wish to take that risk.

TABLE #7
TOTAL VALUES OF EACH ALTERNATIVE AT AGE 70

Buy term	
Cash value	0
Less premiums	$24,040
Net benefits	($24,040)
Buy permanent	
Cash value	$35,364
Less premiums	8,768
Net benefits	$26,596
Gain from buying permanent	$26,596
	(24,040)
	$50,636

When should you buy insurance?

Many people understandably tend to put off getting insurance until some time in the future when they expect their cash flow to be better than it is right now. But once you know you are going to need it some time in the future, the time to buy is right now. There are two reasons: first, you might become uninsurable before you apply (not only by contracting a disease like cancer, but hazardous occupations and hobbies can make you uninsurable as well); second, it will start to cost a great deal more, the longer you put it off.

Table #8 demonstrates the effect of age on total premiums paid by a male non-smoker for term and permanent insurance, based on rates currently in effect for a large insurance company.

Comparative analysis including net present value calculations also indicates the cost-effectiveness of permanent insurance over term in the long run.

TABLE #8
AGE/PREMIUM RELATIONSHIP FOR A MALE NON-SMOKER

Current age	Initial annual premium for $100,000 permanent insurance	Number of years until premiums are paid by dividends	Total permanent insurance premiums paid to age 70	Cash value of permanent insurance at age 70	Net benefit of permanent insurance at age 70 (cash value less premiums paid)	Initial annual premium for $100,000 term insurance to age 70	Number of years to age 70	Total term insurance premiums paid to age 70
30	$461	19	$8,768	$35,364	$26,596	155	40	$24,040
40	773	19	14,679	34,326	19,647	219	30	22,405
50	1,313	24	26,266	30,526	4,260	468	20	19,705
60	2,520	20	25,205	17,087	(8,118)	1,049	10	13,935

57

CONVERTING CAPITAL INTO INCOME

Maximizing capital growth

Major financial decisions at retirement are —

(a) Selection of registered pension income options

(b) Converting non-registered capital into income

(c) Maximizing estate growth through wise financial management

(Again, you will want some professional assistance at this stage of your planning.)

ESTATE PLANNING AND MANAGEMENT

Updating your will

Your estate plan determines your estate's distribution after your death. It also determines the degree of liquidity that the estate will require to pay expenses, taxes, outstanding liabilities, etc., and it makes provision for payment of these expenses.

If you don't have a will, stop reading now, call you lawyer, and get one drawn up. A proper will ensures that *your* will and not the government's prevails when you die. (The government has a will already written for anyone who does not have one of their own and many people will find the terms of the government's all-purpose estate package unacceptable.) Changes in family composition, tax laws, estate law, as well as to your estate itself, require that you call your lawyer or estate planner from time to time to see if your will needs updating.

Before you begin planning your estate, make yourself familiar with the taxes you might be liable for on your death. Capital gains taxes are the first consideration. When you die, if the estate does not go to a surviving spouse, the tax department will deem the assets to have been sold at fair market value and will tax them accordingly. This can cause a severe liquidity shortage and precipitate the untimely sale of assets at much below fair market value. (Not only do the heirs not receive an estate intact, which might be an operating business or real estate, but they almost never receive fair value from the forced sale of the estate.)

If you own an asset that is growing in value, you can elect to "freeze" it and transfer the potential growth to an heir today, rather than waiting until the year of death. This is one way to minimize capital gains tax liabilities in the year of death. However, you should know that today's increasing life expectancies, along with volatile inflation rates, are giving planners some concern. They are now much more conservative in recommending estate freezes.

Estate taxes

Sound estate planning includes a cost-benefit analysis of the four alternative ways of paying the tax:

(a) Use cash from the estate to pay tax. Cost of paying each dollar of tax liability: $1.

(b) Borrow funds to pay tax. Cost of paying each dollar of tax: $1 principal + $1 interest (for example) = $2. For example, if you pay off a $100,000 loan over 15 years at 11%, you will end up repaying $100,000 in principal and $102,000 in interest by monthly payments of $1,121.

(c) Fund tax liability with tax-free life insurance proceeds. Cost of paying each dollar of tax liability: for example, 2¢ to 5¢ per year for 8 years. For example, the cost of $250,000 of permanent insurance for a 46-year-old male non-smoker was recently $7,013 per annum, or 2.8¢ per $1 of insurance for 10 years, at which time the dividends will cover the cost of further premiums. Even if heirs wish to sell the assets, sufficient insurance proceeds will allow them time to sell to take maximum advantage of economic cycles in the marketplace.

(d) Sell all or part of the assets such as real estate or a business interest to fund the tax liability. Cost of paying each dollar of tax liability: $1.25 to $1.50 if markets are strong (extra cost is due to selling expenses and forced sale penalties), or $1.50 to $2.00 if markets are weak and sacrifice sales are necessary.

PLANNED CHARITABLE GIVING

Many of our charitable organizations are private bodies dependent on private contributions. It is also the custom of many people to remember charitable organizations of their choice in their wills. There are many benefits to the donor as well as the donee from a well-designed, planned giving program.

Charitable giving should not come about haphazardly if you are trying to make a plan for your life. Treat it like any other part of your financial life: in stages and in relation to the other components of your plan.

Establish levels of giving

First, complete Worksheet #17 in Part III to determine your planned giving. (You might be surprised to find that you are in a stronger position to support a favored cause than you thought you were. It will then be possible for a personal financial planning/planned giving professional to help you design a plan that most effectively accomplishes both the donor's and the donee's objectives.

Maximize tax benefits and "leverage" using life insurance

You may want to leave a charitable organization a significant gift and at the same time not deprive your heirs of a reasonable inheritance. These two goals can be accomplished by purchasing life insurance on your own life, paying the insurance premiums, and naming the charitable organization as the beneficiary. The insurance can be set up so that the monthly or annual premium payments are deductible from your taxable income. After five or six annual payments, the policy is in force for the duration of your life and no further payments need be made. You may also make one lump sum payment that will pay future insurance premiums.

Most charitable organizations are very much in favor of this kind of giving. The organization has access to the cash values in this insurance as it builds up. Within 30 days of the donor's death the organization will receive the death benefits without delay. Owners can, through their corporations, set up split dollar insurance programs that enable the corporation to pay the bulk of the premiums with the benefits going to the charitable organization so that there is minimal cash loss incurred by the corporation.

The advantages of using life insurance are —

(a) Small monthly tax deductible payments

(b) Gift will not dilute inheritance of heirs

(c) Non-profit organization receives insurance benefits quickly and without problems

If you require a monthly life income, the non-profit organization can take property as a gift, issue a receipt, and, in return, make monthly payments to you by means of a life or term-certain annuity.

A gift of existing life insurance (i.e., insurance that you no longer need) can be made to a charitable organization with a tax receipt being issued for the amount of the cash value of the policy.

Other tax-advantaged vehicles

Through effective tax planning it is possible to give charitable gifts in such a way that the major cost is borne by the government: gifts that are made up of tax-saved dollars that would have otherwise been sent to federal coffers. Taking full advantage of the available deductions for charitable gifts makes good sense for the donor and the charity.

Structure your bequests so that you and your estate are able to take full advantage of the tax breaks for charitable gifts. If you can manage, begin giving additional gifts to your charity throughout your life expectancy to take full advantage of the available tax savings.

If you own valuable property such as a house, you could donate it by means of a charitable remainder trust. The property is given to the charity today but the donors retain the right to use the property until death. The donors receive an immediate charitable gift receipt for tax purposes in the amount of the residual value of the property.

There are many innovative ways of achieving your personal, estate, and planned giving objectives. Professional consultation is recommended in this highly specialized field. A well-designed program can be of significant benefit to you, your estate, and your favorite charities.

CLOSELY HELD BUSINESSES AND PROFESSIONAL CORPORATIONS

Your business exists to accomplish your personal goals. Long-range and business planning can only be done in the context of your personal long-range plans. In a partnership or other corporate group, everyone should try to establish his or her own personal goals, and then together determine the common denominators (among partners). The business' long-range goals should be set to accomplish the personal goals that have been identified.

Relate long-range corporate goals to your personal goals

If you are including corporate or business goals in your life plan, then you should go through a goal-setting process for the corporation similar to the one you are doing for yourself. Again, use the 5-, 10-, and 15-year time frame.

Some business owners and professionals prefer to accumulate sufficient capital (registered and non-registered) to fund their retirement income, independent of the value of their business at retirement. The advantages of this plan are the following:

(a) Regardless of the business's value at retirement, they will enjoy a comfortable standard of living for the rest of their lives

(b) It reduces anxiety, tension, etc., making it easier to run the business effectively and to enjoy pre-retirement life much more. (On the other hand, some prefer the stimulation of the "make-it-or-break-it" challenge.)

(c) It preserves the business entity, which can then be bequeathed by will.

For 1988, in a money-purchase pension program, your company can contribute up to $4,750 toward your retirement capital accumulation program annually. You, as employee, can in turn contribute the same amount providing that you have qualifying income. This provides a total of $4,750 in any given year, compared to the current individual $9,500 RRSP contribution ceiling.

Canadian pension programs

Another available option is the vesting schedule, where company contributions do not vest for a certain period of time and allow the employer to induce key employees to remain with the firm. Employees should consider the interest rate applicable to personal contributions if they retire or resign and compare this to available RRSP rates.

The rules regarding defined benefit plans can be very complex and are constantly changing, and it is best to consult your payroll office to receive current information on a defined benefit plan.

The current RPP and RRSP limits are as follows:

1988: The lesser of $9,500 or 18% of 1987 earned income

1989: The lesser of $11,500 or 18% of 1988 earned income

1990: The lesser of $13,500 or 18% of 1989 earned income

1991: The lesser of $15,500 or 18% of 1990 earned income

For example, an individual in 1988 who earned $40,000 in 1987 would be able to contribute $7,200 (18% of $40,000). To be eligible for the maximum contribution of $9,500, that person must have earned in excess of $52,778 in 1987.

There are, however, a number of proposed changes to the current contribution schedule under consideration, and, therefore, it is advisable to obtain the most up-to-date information.

The rules for U.S. pension programs are even more diverse, and they cover a broad range of topics. For the individual, there are many contribution rules and investment options for the IRA. An employer can offer 401(k), SEP, ESOP, and defined benefit plans, and a self-employed person should be familiar with the rules for Keogh plans.

U.S. pension programs

Depending on which of the above (and in what combination) are applicable to your situation, consult recent government regulations before making any contributions.

Another way to accumulate capital is to increase the capital value of your business for eventual sale. The value of the business may be derived from its ability to generate income and/or from the market value of the company's assets minus its liabilities.

Structuring for sale

It is very important to think about this matter carefully, establish your goals in terms of dollars and time, then design and implement a strategy to accomplish your objectives. If your plan is to eventually sell your business, it is normally a good idea to keep it cash lean, making it easier for a purchaser to finance the acquisition. It is also better for you, the vendor, to have transferred as much cash as possible out of your company into your personal account or into another one of your companies, diversifying your holdings and minimizing the problems created if there is a reversal in the sale.

Many business owners use *inter vivos* buy back agreements to sell their businesses to key employees on an installment plan. The key to these agreements is —

(a) making sure the down payment is substantial, and

(b) in the event of the death of the vendor, prior to being paid out, having sufficient life insurance on his or her life to retire the debt, relieving the estate of having to deal with the purchasers of the business in case there are any problems or difficulties.

Buy/sell agreements

In businesses with two or more owners, buy/sell agreements are essential and these agreements must be adequately funded. If the agreement is arranged before the death or disability of a shareholder, it can be reasonably priced and straightforward. A comprehensive buy/sell agreement defines what will happen in the event of death or disability of a partner, an irreconcilable disagreement by partners and a decision to terminate the partnership, or the voluntary withdrawal of a partner from the business. Buy/sell agreements not only specify how the buy out of a deceased shareholder or partner will occur, but they also specify how the buy out will be funded, particularly in the event of a death or a disability.

Buy/sell agreements can be funded by liquid reserves but they are more usually funded by life insurance and/or disability buy out insurance. The agreement itself should state that the sale price will be reviewed and updated annually, and that appropriate insurance be kept in place. A great variety of insurance contracts are available for such funding. If it appears that the business will be operating for a long time, permanent insurance contracts can be the most cost effective. Split dollar contracts are common, with premiums being paid by the individuals initially, and later by the business. Shareholders or partners in a business often devote the majority of their life's work to the business, and, therefore, it is critically important for their dependents, in particular, to make sure that there is an adequate, well-funded buy/sell agreement in place.

There are many permutations and combinations of funding buy/sell agreements, including the use of disability buy out insurance in the event of the disability of a partner or shareholder. The four alternatives listed for funding estate capital gains taxes also available for funding buy outs.

Additional complications exist for the deceased's estate as well as the surviving shareholders, depending on the ownership percentages and relative financial strength of all parties involved if funding provisions have not been made in advance. An example of buy/sell insurance would be an operating company that buys insurance on the lives of the two shareholders, each in the amount of the value of each shareholder's interest in the business.

When one shareholder dies the company receives the insurance proceeds, buys the deceased shareholder's shares back from the estate, and then redeems the shares.

If the two shareholders each own one half of a company that has a total value of $250,000, the company would purchase $125,000 insurance on each of the partners' lives. When one shareholder dies, the company receives the $125,000 insurance proceeds which it then pays to the deceased partner's estate to redeem his or her shares in the company.

The estate then nets $125,000 less the applicable capital gains tax. The company has the same cash position as before. The number of company shares outstanding is reduced by 50% and the surviving shareholder owns 100% of the company's earning capacity.

Part III
MAKING YOUR OWN PLAN

When you have successfully completed this section of the book, you will have an integrated working personal financial plan: a detailed statement of your goals and a personalized action plan with start and completion dates specifying —

(a) what you are going to do,

(b) when you are going to do it,

(c) how you are going to do it,

(d) where you are going to do it, and

(e) who will do each task for the achievement of each of your goals.

In this section, I refer to Parts I and II for clarification and information as required.

THE PROCESS

As you develop your goals and plans and estimate the cost of achieving each, you will modify your projected expenses and income accordingly. You will find yourself making trade-offs and choices between present and future costs and benefits.

When you have finalized your plan, review each of your goals, concerns, and "things to-do" worksheets; then write down on your calendar the start-up and completion dates of each activity noted.

You will also have a schedule for updating your plan on a regular basis and at each financially significant event in your life. After you have determined your goals, you will do an analysis of your income and expenses and project future income and expenses (using selected inflation factors and financial independence ages of your choice). From this point you can then estimate your annual surpluses or deficits. The surpluses will be used to accumulate capital, which can then be converted into income to fund your deficits after your anticipated age at financial independence. You can also do the necessary projections to determine the capital necessary to fund future family living expenses in case your employment or business income is prematurely terminated due to death, disability, or business failure.

Estimating the capital you require for financial independence is another critical step in your planning process. The tables and graphs illustrated in Part II show the capital required at various ages to generate a given level of after-tax to help you estimate your capital requirements.

Next, you will consider the best alternative strategies for achieving your capital accumulation objectives. Once you decide on your optimal plan, you can then make detailed plans for its implementation and carry them out.

CONVERTING CAPITAL INTO INCOME

You will also plan for conversion of your capital into income. This is a step that is almost completely neglected by many people who are at, in, or near retirement. Years of hard work and disciplined capital accumulation can be wasted by a hasty stroke of the pen in the process of converting capital into income. This involves decisions regarding pensions, annuities, and the use of bonds, stocks, and other assets as sources of retirement income.

Your next step will be to double check each step of your plan and see if it is still congruent with your goals and preferences. You should also review Part II to see if there are some improvements that you can make in the financial instruments that you have selected to accumulate your capital and to convert it into income.

REVIEW AND UPDATE

After having drawn up your schedule of "what you need to do and when you need to do it" to implement your plan, make sure that you follow your schedule to the letter. Reviewing and updating your plan annually is also fundamentally important to a successful personal financial planning process.

Depending on your age, health, current financial status, etc., some parts of the planning process may be more important to you than others. If this is the case, then emphasize those parts of greatest relevance to you, but make sure that you are familiar with each phase of the process. You don't want to ignore an aspect that in hindsight might be of considerable importance to your financial program.

The many worksheets provided in this section are intended for your use. But you may want to photocopy them before filling them in for the first time. You'll no doubt want to make changes on some of them as you proceed. Appendix 6 also includes forms for recording personal information, a description of personal property, and the location of important documents.

CREATING YOUR GOALS: THE FOUNDATION

This is the map-making stage. It will set the direction of your entire financial plan. Take the time to do it well.

Life goals

Review and do the goal development process described on page 24. If you find the exercises difficult, then proceed directly to the goal worksheets below.

If you do the planning exercises as described in Part II, write down, in as much detail as possible, each area of your life that is highly motivating: one year and five years from now, and at your age of financial independence as well as throughout financial independence. This process ensures that your emotional life is part of the planning process. It's also a good idea to double check all of your goals with how you "feel" about accomplishing each. If your "feelings" contradict your logical, rational, deductive processes, then you are well advised to go back to the drawing board and reconsider your goals until they "feel" right and are highly motivating, as well as being logical and rational.

Read through the following example, then complete your own goals worksheet.

Define your personal financial goals

Goal: To generate sufficient after-tax income to equal or exceed the total projected expenses up to financial independence.

Plan: My projected after-tax employment income exceeds my projected expenses;

OR

Plan: My projected annual after-tax employment income exceeds my projected expenses with the exception of funding a trip to Europe in four years and funding university expenses for my daughter, Mary.

To fund these two expenses, the following are my goals and plans:

Goal: To travel to Europe in four years at an anticipated expense of $10,000.

Plan: To save $1,600 per year indexed at 5% per year, earning 10% per year (after tax), commencing immediately. After adding this expense to my projected expenses, my projected after-tax income still exceeds my projected expenses.

Goal: To fund 50% of Mary's university expenses, estimated to be $5,000 per year x 0.5 = $2,500 per year for four years, indexed at 5%, commencing in two years.

Plan: To save $2,000 per year commencing in one year for four years, earning 10% per year (after tax).

After adding this expense to my projected expenses my projected after-tax income still exceeds my projected expenses.

Note: If projected income is less than projected expenses then —

(a) other expenses must be reduced accordingly,

(b) the goal must be reduced accordingly,

(c) income must increase, or

(d) a combination of (a), (b), and (c).

Now complete the Goal Worksheets (see Worksheets #3 to #7).

Listed below are some common personal financial goals. If the goal is a priority for you mark X under Y(es), if it isn't mark X under N(o). After each goal marked Y, complete a detailed goal description specifying dollar amounts, when you want to accomplish the goal, and other relevant details (see Worksheet #4).

	Y	N
Maintain my current standard of living	❑	❑
Improve my current standard of living	❑	❑
Improve my future standard of living	❑	❑
Financial independence at age _____	❑	❑
Support of charitable or social cause	❑	❑
Support of parents or in-laws	❑	❑
College education for children	❑	❑
Vacation home or expensive recreational vehicle/vessel	❑	❑
Extraordinary travel	❑	❑
Education of self or spouse	❑	❑
Support of surviving (dependent) spouse	❑	❑
Transfer ownership of business enterprise to others	❑	❑
Other_____	❑	❑
_____	❑	❑
_____	❑	❑
_____	❑	❑
_____	❑	❑

WORKSHEET #4
DETAILED GOAL DESCRIPTION

For each of your financial goals you included on Worksheet #3, clearly specify dollar amounts, when you want to achieve the goal, where and how it will be done, and who will do it.

My specific goal is —

This is what needs to be done to accomplish the goal:

This is my plan and schedule for accomplishing the goal:

My specific goal is —

This is what needs to be done to accomplish the goal:

This is my plan and schedule for accomplishing the goal:

My specific goal is —

This is what needs to be done to accomplish the goal:

This is my plan and schedule for accomplishing the goal:

My specific goal is —

This is what needs to be done to accomplish the goal:

This is my plan and schedule for accomplishing the goal:

This is a list of common financial concerns and things that many people want to do but because of procrastination or other causes have not yet done. Mark Y(es) if it is a concern and something you will take action on, and N(o) if it isn't.

	Y	N
Simplify my cash management	❏	❏
Increase my cash flow for ordinary expenditures	❏	❏
Increase my cash flow for unusual expenditures	❏	❏
Build an emergency cash reserve	❏	❏
Reduce or consolidate my existing debt	❏	❏
Select investment targets for my portfolio	❏	❏
Learn how to evaluate potential investment opportunities	❏	❏
Learn how to better manage existing investments	❏	❏
Catch up on prior years' taxes	❏	❏
Determine my need for life insurance	❏	❏
Determine my need for disability insurance	❏	❏
Purchase the "right" life insurance package	❏	❏
Purchase adequate disability insurance	❏	❏
Reduce potential taxes arising at death	❏	❏
Prepare or re-draft my will	❏	❏
Provide greater security for my heirs on death	❏	❏
Ensure continuity of my business at time of retirement, death, or disability	❏	❏
Find a financial adviser	❏	❏
Coordinate my planning with my financial adviser(s)	❏	❏
Keep adequate financial records	❏	❏
Simplify my bookkeeping	❏	❏
Embark on a regular savings program	❏	❏
Achieve peace of mind concerning my financial condition	❏	❏
Protect myself against financial loss	❏	❏

For every Y(es) you have marked, complete a Concerns and "To Do" Planning Worksheet (see Worksheet #7).

MARK YES OR NO:	Y	N
Change or modify career activities	❏	❏
Change or modify family and social activities (e.g., marriage or divorce)	❏	❏
Change or modify nature of business activities	❏	❏
Transfer ownership of business enterprise to others	❏	❏
Support of charitable or social cause	❏	❏
Major health problems that currently exist	❏	❏
Value of assets that have a very wide potential high/low spread	❏	❏
Outstanding tax problems	❏	❏
Inheritance	❏	❏
Going into own business	❏	❏
Other _____	❏	❏
_____	❏	❏
_____	❏	❏
_____	❏	❏
_____	❏	❏

Note: Review your entire Personal Financial Program when any of the factors noted above become predictable and/or definite.

CONCERNS AND "TO DO" PLANNING WORKSHEET

I know that I will have *(specify what it is you want to do)* _____

_____

when I have *(describe what it is that you will have done when you have accomplished the task)*

_____

_____

THIS IS MY PLAN AND SCHEDULE FOR COMPLETING THE TASK

_____

_____

_____

_____

_____

_____

_____

_____

_____

_____

Clearly specify — What will be done
　　　　　　　　— When it will be done (include start and completion dates)
　　　　　　　　— Where it will be done
　　　　　　　　— How it will be done
　　　　　　　　— Who will do it

Now establish your present financial position with a list of your assets and liabilities. From this you can determine your present net worth. Net worth is fundamentally important because it represents the amount available for investment or conversion into income.

YOUR CURRENT AND FUTURE STANDARD OF LIVING

Your net worth is your assets minus your liabilities. For your purposes, subtract the value of your residence and personal property from this figure to estimate the capital available for investment. Then calculate the capital you need to fund any potential future income loss due to death, disability, business failure, etc., as well as the capital required for financial independence.

Your personal balance sheet

If you plan to sell your present home eventually and replace it with one of less value at financial independence, the difference between the two will be added in to the capital you will have available at financial independence. (See Worksheet #8.)

Worksheet #9 is a schedule of personal expenses. Filling in this form may take some time. If you haven't been keeping track of your personal expenditures over the past year, you'll have to work backwards from your checkbook and charge account receipts and estimate cash expenditures to make an accurate accounting. It will be worth your trouble to do so.

Current living expenses

This schedule is a key building block of your overall plan. From it you will build the projection of future expenses, which will effectively give you a budget for those years.

Having established your actual expenses for the past year, you are ready to project your future expenditures. (See Worksheet #10.) This stage requires some re-thinking and a lot of careful planning, so take your time. Look at each category of expense in your Worksheet #9, and estimate any significant deviations that will occur in future for extraordinary expenses such as education, travel, and recreational property. Multiplying total personal expenditure in current dollars by the appropriate inflation factor from the inflation table in Appendix 3, you can calculate your total personal expenditure in future dollars. Note how much inflation increases your cash requirement to meet living expenses each year.

Future living expenses to retirement

73

WORKSHEET #8
PERSONAL BALANCE SHEET

STATEMENT OF ASSETS AND LIABILITIES

AS AT _____ ,19 _____

	Current market value
Assets	
Cash in bank accounts	$ _____
Term deposits	_____
Bonds	_____
Loans and notes receivable	_____
Public company stocks and mutual funds	_____
Cash surrender value of life insurance (Coverage $ _____)	_____
Residence	_____
Less: Mortgage(s)	(_____)
RRSPs, IRAs, etc.	_____
Value of employer deferred compensation plans (pension, profit sharing, stock options)	_____
Vacation home	_____
Less: Mortgage(s)	(_____)
Other real estate holdings net of mortgage obligations	_____
Business interests — at cost (Market value $ _____)	_____
Automobile(s)	_____
Personal property	_____
Other	_____
Total assets	_____
Liabilities	
Unpaid bills owing	$ _____
Income taxes payable	_____
Loans payable	_____
_____	
_____	
_____	
Insurance policy loans	_____
Other	_____
Total liabilities	$ _____
Net Worth	$ _____
Residence Less Mortgage(s) + Automobile(s) + Personal Property	$ _____
Net Worth excluding Residence Less Mortgage(s), Automobile(s) and Personal Property (Capital available for investment or conversion into income)	$ _____

WORKSHEET #9
PERSONAL EXPENSES
FOR THE PAST CALENDAR YEAR 19___

	Regular expenses	Extra-ordinary expenses	Total expenses
Housing			
Rent/mortgage payments			
Property taxes			
Heating			
Electricity			
Insurance			
Maintenance and improvements			
Furnishings and appliances			
Telephone			
Water			
TV rental or cable			
Other			
Food			
At home			
Away			
Transportation			
Public transportation			
Automobile			
— Car payments/rentals			
— Gas and oil			
— Insurance			
— License			
— Repairs and maintenance			
— Tires			
Clothing			
Purchases			
Laundry and cleaning			
Recreation, reading, and education			
Travel and vacation			
Recreational property			

	Regular expenses	Extra-ordinary expenses	Total expenses
Recreation, continued			
Club memberships and dues			
Miscellaneous entertainment			
Babysitting (non-deductible)			
Education			
— Tuition			
— Books			
— Miscellaneous			
Reading material			
Tobacco and alcohol			
Tobacco			
Alcohol			
Health and personal care			
Medicine and medical services not covered by insurance			
Medical and dental insurance premiums			
Dental care not covered by insurance			
Grooming			
Insurance premiums			
Life			
Disability			
Liability			
Other _____			
Other			
Charitable donations			
Gifts to friends and family			
Other_____			
Total personal expenditures			

WORKSHEET #10
PROJECTED PERSONAL EXPENSES FROM THE
CURRENT CALENDAR YEAR UNTIL RETIREMENT

Age	Total personal expenditure from base year (from schedule of personal expenses) (Current $)	Adjustments for extraordinary expenses or changes in living standard* (Current $)	Total personal expenditure (Current $)	Inflation**		Total personal expenditure (Future $)
				Rate	Factor	

* Note expenses such as mortgage payments and permanent insurance premiums that will be fully paid within a specific period and reduce projected expenses accordingly

** From inflation table (see Appendix 3).

Future disposable income until retirement

Use Worksheet #11 to estimate your present disposable income. Then use Worksheet #12 to project your disposable income for future years. The yearly disposable income figure from Worksheet #11 is placed in the total income from base year column of Worksheet #12 for each year from your current age until your retirement age. If any significant deviations in disposable income are expected in future years, these should be recorded in the adjustments column. Such adjustments could be required for expected leaves of absence, large salary increases, reduced investment income, etc. Disposable income in current dollars is then multiplied by the appropriate inflation factor from the inflation table in Appendix 3 to arrive at disposable income in future dollars.

Net income

Subtracting total personal expenditure in future dollars from Worksheet #12 leaves your net income after expenses in future dollars.

Adjust the income and expense projection

A quick look at the totals of your income and expense columns will tell you whether you should go back and rework some of your numbers. You must develop an income that exceeds, or is equal to, your expenses. If this is the case, you can proceed to the next step. If not, go back to the drawing board and redo your worksheet.

After doing the next steps, you may find that your income and expense projection is still not satisfactory, and you may have to rework it again. Until your plan is finalized, you will be constantly modifying your income and expense projections. Future income and financial benefits for you or others carry a price tag. If the price tag is too large, then future income and financial benefits projections must be reduced to reduce current and future costs, resulting in lower expenditures. This back and forth is an essential part of the planning process — choosing between current and future costs, and current and future benefits.

WORKSHEET #11
DISPOSABLE INCOME FOR THE CALENDAR YEAR 19___

	Monthly	Yearly
Salary and bonuses		
Interest, dividends, and capital gains		
Other income		
Total income		
Deduct personal taxes & other deductions at source		
Disposable income		

WORKSHEET #12
PROJECTED DISPOSABLE INCOME AND NET INCOME
FROM THE CURRENT CALENDAR YEAR
UNTIL RETIREMENT

Age	Disposable income from base year (from schedule of income) (current $)	Adjustments for extraordinary income or other changes* (current $)	Disposable income (current $)	Inflation**		Disposable income (future $)	Total personal expenditure (future $) (from schedule of projected personal expenses)	Net income after expenses (future $)
				Rate	Factor			

*   Include in extraordinary income anticipated inheritances, profits from sale of property, receipts of mortgage payments, etc.

** From inflation table (see Appendix 3).

79

PROTECT YOUR STANDARD OF LIVING

Now that you've established a standard of living, you must take steps to protect it in the event of disability, unemployment, business failure, premature death, or to protect your spouse or your heirs.

As it is apparent that the government is unable to support most people in the standard of living they wish, for full protection, tailor-made private insurance plans are the best option.

For graphic illustrations of the accumulation and depletion of capital from now throughout life expectancy, refer to the insurance graphs starting on page 48.

Use Worksheets #13 and #14 and Table #9 to calculate your insurance needs. Then move on to Worksheet #15 to state your financial independence objectives.

WORKSHEET #13
DISABILITY INCOME INSURANCE PLAN

A. Annual personal expenditure:
(from Schedule of Personal Expenses) _____

B. Sources of annual non-employment income

Spouse's income _____

Government disability benefits _____

Disability benefits from work _____

Income from income-producing assets
(from Schedule of Disposable Income) _____

Other income
(from Schedule of Disposable Income) _____

TOTAL ANNUAL NON-EMPLOYMENT INCOME _____

C. Additional annual disability income insurance needed
(subtract B from A) _____

THIS IS MY PLAN:

I will obtain $ _____ of disability income insurance

This is who I will contact _____

_____

This is when I will do it _____

Note: Lump sum disability insurance benefits are available instead of monthly benefits and if this option is selected, the lump sum coverage required would be calculated in the same way that life insurance needs are calculated (see Table #9).

TABLE #9
LIFE INSURANCE REQUIRED TO FUND
SURVIVOR'S ANNUAL EXPENDITURES

Age of insured	Annual living expenses (current $)	Capital required to fund unfunded living expenses
30	$10,000	$549,386
35	10,000	504,477
40	10,000	458,987
45	10,000	413,213
50	10,000	366,889
55	10,000	320,242
60	10,000	272,936
65	10,000	225,336
70	10,000	177,107

Assumptions:*

(a) Annual interest rate: 6%
(b) Inflation rate: 4%
(c) Average tax rate: 30%
(d) Surviving spouse's life expectancy: 87
(e) $10,000 (current $) after tax is amount required to meet unfunded living expenses.

*Rough adjustments can be made to the capital required figure when the assumptions above do not hold.

WORKSHEET #14
SURVIVOR INCOME LIFE INSURANCE WORKSHEET

A. Annual personal expenditure
    (from Schedule of Personal Expenses) _____

B. Sources of annual income

    Spouse's income _____

    CPP survivor benefits/Social security _____

    Other sources of income
    excluding investments and life insurance _____

    Total annual income excluding investments and life insurance _____

C. Additional income needed
    (Subtract B from A) _____

D. Total capital required

    To Fund C (additional income needed
    — see Table #9) _____

    Final expenses _____

    Education for children _____

    Liabilities (from personal balance sheet) _____

    Total capital required _____

E. Sources of available capital

    Savings and investments
    (from personal balance sheet) _____

    Proceeds from existing life insurance _____

    Total available capital _____

F. Additional life insurance needed
    (subtract E from D) _____

THIS IS MY PLAN:

    I will obtain $_____ of life insurance.

    This is who I will contact _____

    _____

    This is when I will do it _____

When answering the following questions, consider your requirements in after-tax dollars:

If you were today at the age of your desired financial independence, living the lifestyle you expect to live at that time, what would your expenses be in today's dollars?

$_____ per month $ _____ per year

If you were disabled today for an extended period of time, what would your expenses be in today's dollars?

$_____ per month $ _____ per year

What is the earning capacity of your spouse today in after-tax dollars?

$_____ per month $ _____ per year

If you were to die today, what would your family's expenses be in today's dollars?

$_____ per month $ _____ per year

Your current age: _____   Spouse's current age: _____

Age at financial independence:_____

Projected annual inflation rate_____% per year.

Projected annual increase in investment and employment income _____ % per year.

Estimated average tax rate: _____

This is the amount of unfunded living expenses from my financial independence at age ____ to my life expectancy: $_____

This is the amount of savings required to generate an income sufficient to meet the unfunded living expenses: $_____
(See Figures #9, #10, and #11 in Part II to calculate this figure.)

I will accomplish this savings program by following this plan:

_____

_____

_____

_____

commencing _____

_____

_____

(Use one or more extra pages to describe your savings program.)

CONVERTING NON-REGISTERED CAPITAL

The prescribed annuity or retirement annuity (subject to some limitations) is a good tool for converting non-registered capital into income. For example, consider four people who want a retirement income of $24,000 to age 70. The first two want to retire at age 60 and the other two at age 65.

The first is 57 and he purchases a three-year deferred, ten-year term certain prescribed annuity. He makes the investment now and starts receiving the payments in three years for a ten-year period.

The second is 60 and she purchases an immediate ten-year certain prescribed annuity that pays for the next ten years.

The third is 62 and purchases a three-year deferred, five-year term certain prescribed annuity. He pays the premium now and starts receiving the payments in three years for a five-year period.

The fourth is 65 and she purchases an immediate five-year term certain prescribed annuity which pays for the next five-years. The single premiums required to purchase each of these annuities, based on the current rates offered by a large insurance company, are shown in Table #10.

For example, a 60-year-old person retires and wishes to immediately convert $250,000 of non-registered capital into a level income until age 70, at which time he begins receiving income from registered funds. An annual income of $37,033 will be generated. (See the second example in Table #10: $250,000/162,016 x $24,000 = $37,033.) In practice, you would, of course, make an allowance under living expenses for inflation.

Figures #7 and #8 in Part II illustrate saving with registered versus non-registered programs.

You should now be able to complete the Worksheet #16.

TABLE #10
PRESCRIBED ANNUITY PREMIUMS

Current age	Deferral period (years)	Income payment period ages (inclusive)	Single deposit ($)	Level annual income payments	
				Before tax ($)	After tax*($)
57	3	61 - 70	$116,686	$24,000	$19,683
60	0	61 - 70	162,016	24,000	21,269
62	3	66 - 70	74,489	24,000	20,814
65	0	66 - 70	103,240	24,000	22,826

*Assuming a 35% marginal tax rate

WORKSHEET #16
CAPITAL CONVERSION

Age of financial independence: _____

Number of years from
financial independence to age 71: _____

Average living expenses including taxes over this period: $ _____

Less non-registered sources of income:

         _____ $ _____

         _____ $ _____

         _____ $ _____

Annual income required, indexed at _____ %/year for inflation $ _____

THIS IS MY PLAN TO CONVERT CAPITAL INTO INCOME:

This is who I will contact:_____

         _____

This is when I will do it: _____

Worksheet #17 can be used to plan and monitor immediate and deferred gifts for the future. There are many alternative planned giving strategies. Get competent help; it will assist you and the recipient. Re-read the section in Part II on planned giving.

PLANNED CHARITABLE GIVING

When designing your estate plan, you need to decide if you are going to more or less exhaust your wealth by the time you expect to die, or if you are going to pass on some or all of your wealth to other people and/or charitable organizations.

ESTATE PLAN

Whenever you are determining how the assets of your estate are to be applied and distributed, you must also consider the source of these funds. Will it be liquid assets, non-liquid assets, or insurance proceeds? How will you know that sufficient assets will be available at the time of your death for distribution according to your intentions? If you wish to protect your estate from income tax, final expenses, specific bequests, cash legacies, or in case you live longer than you expect, then permanent life insurance is an appropriate vehicle. Keep it in mind as you complete Worksheet #18.

Year	Age	Projected annual giving		Actual annual giving	
		Immediate	Deferred	Immediate	Deferred

These are the charitable organizations I wish to benefit:

_____

_____

_____

_____

	Y	N
Do I want to give regular tax deductible gifts?	❏	❏
Do I want to give an immediate major gift?	❏	❏
If so, do I want to receive back a monthly income?	❏	❏
Do I want to make a deferred gift?	❏	❏
If so, will it be by testamentary bequest?	❏	❏
– by insurance?	❏	❏
– by other vehicle?_____	❏	❏
Yes, my program includes effective tax planning	❏	❏

THIS IS MY CHARITABLE GIVING PLAN:

This is who I will contact: _____

_____

_____

_____

This is when I will do it: _____

WORKSHEET #18
ESTATE PLAN

My will is dated _____

	Y	N
My will is up to date	☐	☐

My executors are _____

My guardians of minor children are _____

This is what I want to leave (dollar amounts and major assets) to my heirs

_____

_____

_____

_____

The source of money and assets for the above is

_____

_____

_____

_____

To favorite charities

_____

_____

_____

_____

Source of assets for the above is

_____

_____

_____

I anticipate that my estate will be liable for the payment of
$ _____ for income taxes

	Y	N
I want to provide for the payment of these taxes	❏	❏

If yes the source is

_____

_____

I anticipate that my estate will be liable for legal and executor's fees and other final expenses in the amount of $ _____

	Y	N
I want to provide for the payment of these expenses	❏	❏

If yes the source is

_____

_____

Other estate goals (specify)

_____

_____

_____

Plan for accomplishing goals

_____

_____

_____

_____

CLOSELY HELD BUSINESSES AND PROFESSIONAL CORPORATIONS

If you are a business owner or a professional corporation, use Worksheet #19.

WORKSHEET #19
BUSINESS OWNER WORKSHEET

I plan to have sufficient capital to fund my living expenses after financial independence without depending on the value of my business:

YES _____   NO _____

(If NO, are you structuring your business to provide the liquidity you need, when you need it? If so, what is your plan? If not, then commence planning immediately.)

Are you a partner or significant shareholder in a business?

YES _____   NO _____

If YES, do you have an up-to-date buy/sell agreement?

YES _____   NO _____

Is it fully funded with insurance or available liquid assets?

YES _____   NO _____

(If the answer to either of the last two questions is NO, then remedy immediately.)

This is what I will do and when I will do it:

_____

_____

_____

_____

_____

_____

Worksheet #20 enables you to check off the basic elements of your financial plan as they are planned and implemented. **YOUR PERSONAL CHECKLIST**

WORKSHEET #20
PERSONAL FINANCIAL PLANNING CHECKLIST

ITEM	I HAVE PLANNED IT		I HAVE IMPLEMENTED IT	
	YES	NO	YES	NO
Set goals – living expenses – age of financial independence				
Will				
Budget				
Insurance – life – disability				
Buy/sell agreement				
Planned giving				
Tax deferral				
Maximize tax deductions				
Income splitting				
Savings/debt reduction – registered – non-registered				
Investments – registered – non-registered				
Conversion of capital to income				

YOUR FINANCIAL PLANNING CALENDAR

Worksheet #21 enables you to keep track of your plan and reminds you when to implement each step.

As you now know, personal financial planning is a complex and dynamic process. To protect and provide for your future and your dependents' future, it is essential that you put in place a comprehensive and balanced financial plan. Once your plan is implemented, however, you cannot neglect it. It will have to be adjusted from time to time to accommodate changes in interest rates, inflation, insurance and disability income coverage; or you may have to amend your will, as new dependents appear or your goals change. An unexpected inheritance, a career change, a change in your spouse's income — all of these should be reflected in your ongoing personal financial plan. Take the time to review your plan at least once every year and revise it as necessary. When doing so, do not hesitate to seek the advice of a qualified professional financial planner. Once your financial plan is in place you should feel freed up, emotionally as well as financially, to pursue your other life goals.

WORKSHEET #21
PERSONAL FINANCIAL PLANNING CALENDAR BY QUARTER

Year	Jan - Mar	Apr - June	July - Sept	Oct - Dec
19 --				
19 --				
19 --				
19 --				
19 --				

Note: You will need to draw up your own calendar to provide sufficient space for your notes. List each "to do" from the concerns and "to do" planning worksheets in the appropriate quarter above. Include the applicable date. Whenever a new "to do" is established, describe it on a concerns and "to do" planning worksheet and then enter it here. Review this calendar at the beginning of each quarter.

APPENDIX 1

LIFE TABLE 1980-1982

If your current age is	Then the average life expectancy for your age group is	
	Male	Female
30	74.11	80.36
31	74.17	80.39
32	74.22	80.42
33	74.28	80.45
34	74.34	80.48
35	74.39	80.51
36	74.45	80.55
37	74.52	80.59
38	74.58	80.63
39	74.65	80.68
40	74.72	80.73
41	74.80	80.78
42	74.88	80.84
43	74.97	80.90
44	75.06	80.97
45	75.16	81.04
46	75.27	81.11
47	75.39	81.19
48	75.52	81.28
49	75.66	81.37
50	75.81	81.47
51	75.97	81.57
52	76.14	81.68
53	76.33	81.80
54	76.52	81.93
55	76.73	82.06
56	76.95	82.20
57	77.18	82.35
58	77.43	82.51
59	77.69	82.68
60	77.96	82.85
61	78.25	83.03
62	78.56	83.22
63	78.88	83.42
64	79.21	83.63
65	79.57	83.85
66	79.93	84.09
67	80.32	84.33
68	80.72	84.59
69	81.14	84.86
70	81.58	85.14

Source: *Life tables, Canada and province, 1980-82*, Statistics Canada Catalogue 85-532, May, 1984.

APPENDIX 2

PATIENT DAYS BY MAJOR CAUSES,
GENERAL AND ALLIED HOSPITALS, 1980-81

Major cause	Millions of patient days	
	Female	Male
Mental disorders	2.3	1.8
Heart diseases	2.0	1.8
Cerebrovascular diseases	2.1	1.6
Neoplasms - malignant	1.5	1.6
- benign	0.4	0.1
Respiratory diseases	1.2	1.6
Accidents	1.3	1.4
Diseases of the nervous system	1.4	1.1
All deliveries	2.3	0.0
Diseases of the musculoskeletal system	1.4	0.9
Symptoms: senility and ill-defined conditions	0.8	0.6
Arteriosclerotic diseases	0.7	0.5
Diseases of breast and female genitalia	0.9	0.0
Infections of kidney and urinary system	0.8	0.4
Diabetes	0.5	0.3
Infectious diseases	0.3	0.3

Source: *Hospital morbidity 1979-80 and 1980-80*, Statistics Canada Catalogue 82,206, July, 1984.

APPENDIX 3

INFLATION/INTEREST TABLE

Year	INFLATION/INTEREST FACTORS AT YEAR END				
	4%	6%	8%	10%	12%
1	1.04	1.06	1.08	1.10	1.12
2	1.08	1.12	1.17	1.21	1.25
3	1.12	1.19	1.26	1.33	1.40
4	1.17	1.26	1.36	1.46	1.57
5	1.22	1.34	1.47	1.61	1.76
6	1.27	1.42	1.59	1.77	1.97
7	1.32	1.50	1.71	1.95	2.21
8	1.37	1.59	1.85	2.14	2.48
9	1.42	1.69	2.00	2.36	2.77
10	1.48	1.79	2.16	2.59	3.11
11	1.54	1.90	2.33	2.85	3.48
12	1.60	2.01	2.52	3.14	3.90
13	1.67	2.13	2.72	3.45	4.36
14	1.73	2.26	2.94	3.80	4.89
15	1.80	2.40	3.17	4.18	5.47
16	1.87	2.54	3.43	4.59	6.13
17	1.95	2.69	3.70	5.05	6.87
18	2.03	2.85	4.00	5.56	7.69
19	2.11	3.03	4.32	6.12	8.61
20	2.19	3.21	4.66	6.73	9.65
21	2.28	3.40	5.03	7.40	10.80
22	2.37	3.60	5.44	8.14	12.10
23	2.46	3.82	5.87	8.95	13.55
24	2.56	4.05	6.34	9.85	15.18
25	2.67	4.29	6.85	10.83	17.00
26	2.77	4.55	7.40	11.92	19.04
27	2.88	4.82	7.99	13.11	21.32
28	3.00	5.11	8.63	14.42	23.88
29	3.12	5.42	9.32	15.86	26.75
30	3.24	5.74	10.06	17.45	29.96
31	3.37	6.09	10.87	19.19	33.56
32	3.51	6.45	11.74	21.11	37.58
33	3.65	6.84	12.68	23.23	42.09
34	3.79	7.25	13.69	25.55	47.14
35	3.95	7.69	14.79	28.10	52.80
36	4.10	8.15	15.97	30.91	59.14
37	4.27	8.64	17.25	34.00	66.23
38	4.44	9.15	18.63	37.40	74.18
39	4.62	9.70	20.12	41.14	83.08
40	4.80	10.29	21.72	45.26	93.05
41	4.99	10.90	23.46	49.79	104.22
42	5.19	11.56	25.34	54.76	116.72
43	5.40	12.25	27.37	60.24	130.73
44	5.62	12.99	29.56	66.26	146.42
45	5.84	13.76	31.92	72.89	163.99
46	6.07	14.59	34.47	80.18	183.67
47	6.32	15.47	37.23	88.20	205.71
48	6.57	16.39	40.21	97.02	230.39
49	6.83	17.38	43.43	106.72	258.04
50	7.11	18.42	46.90	117.39	289.00
51	7.39	19.53	50.65	129.13	323.68
52	7.69	20.70	54.71	142.04	362.52
53	7.99	21.94	59.08	156.25	406.03
54	8.31	23.26	63.81	171.87	454.75
55	8.65	24.65	68.91	189.06	509.32
56	8.99	26.13	74.43	207.97	570.44
57	9.35	27.70	80.38	228.76	638.89
58	9.73	29.36	86.81	251.64	715.56
59	10.12	31.12	93.76	276.80	801.43

APPENDIX 4

ESTIMATING INCOME TAX RATES

CANADA

The following table provides a rough illustration of the combined federal and provincial taxes payable for residents of British Columbia and Ontario in 1987. This chart will be adequate for most long-term projections as a means of providing an appropriate marginal tax rate figure; for a more precise figure and for specific rates for other provinces, refer to your tax return from last year.

COMBINED FEDERAL AND PROVINCIAL PERSONAL INCOME TAX RATES*					
Taxable income		Ontario	50%	B.C.	51.5%
Lower limit	Upper limit	Basic tax	Rate on excess	Basic tax	Rate on excess
$0	$1,320	$0	6.18%	$0	9.27%
1,320	1,861	81	16.48	122	24.27
1,861	2,075	170	16.40	256	24.27
2,075	2,135	206	74.48	309	24.27
2,135	2,275	250	74.48	324	24.27
2,275	2,639	355	24.48	358	24.27
2,639	4,197	444	26.01	448	26.27
4,197	5,279	849	26.01	857	26.27
5,279	5,780	1,131	27.54	1,142	27.81
5,780	7,918	1,269	27.54	1,281	27.81
7,918	9,780	1,857	29.07	1,876	29.36
9,780	10,524	2,399	29.07	2,422	29.36
10,524	13,197	2,615	29.07	2,641	29.36
13,197	16,880	3,392	30.60	3,425	30.90
16,880	18,476	4,519	30.60	4,563	30.90
18,476	23,755	5,008	35.19	5,057	35.54
23,755	25,000	6,865	38.25	6,932	38.63
25,000	33,304	7,341	38.25	7,413	38.63
33,304	35,915	10,518	38.25	10,621	38.63
35,915	36,952	11,516	38.25	11,629	38.63
36,952	44,332	11,913	45.90	12,029	46.35
44,332	63,347	15,300	46.35	15,450	46.35
63,347	and up	24,114	52.53	24,264	52.53

* The rates include federal tax, the 3% federal surtax, provincial tax at the rates indicated, and any provincial adjustments for surtaxes, flat taxes, or reductions. The rates reflect budget proposals to July 31, 1987. Where tax is determined under the minimum tax provisions, the above table is not applicable.

Note: The new general anti-avoidance rule is expected to be in place by the end of 1987. This is a catch-all that says if you don't break any rules, you can still be charged with "intention to circumvent the system." It is estimated that it will be seven years or more of judicial interpretation before informed counsel can be given on whether or not a specific "tax plan" will be caught by this rule.

UNITED STATES

With the introduction of the Tax Reform Act, a single taxpayer in 1988 can follow these guidelines for calculating the federal marginal bracket:

Taxable Income		Taxes Payable	
From	To	Basic tax	Rate on excess
$0	$17,850	$0	15%
17,851	43,150	2,686	28
43,151	89,560	9,762	33
89,561	+	25,077	27*

* A 5% surcharge is applicable to taxpayers earnings in excess of $89,560 that removes the benefit of any personal exemptions claimed. The maximum surcharge is based on the number of exemptions claimed at $546 per exemption.

To determine the amount of state taxes payable, base your calculations on the tables provide in last year's tax return.

APPENDIX 5

INTESTATE SUCCESSION
(How your estate will be distributed if you die without a will)

All to spouse

1. If you leave a spouse and no issue

1/2 of remainder to spouse

First $75,000 to spouse*

1/2 of remainder to child*

2. If you leave a spouse and one child or issue

1/3 of remainder to spouse

First $75,000 to spouse*

2/3 of remainder equally among children

3. If you leave a spouse and two or more children or issue

All to child or equally among children

4. If you leave a child or children only, or issue, but no spouse

---

(a) to father and mother or survivor

(b) if neither survives, to brothers and sisters with children of deceased brother or sister taking parent's share

(c) if none survive, to nieces and nephews without representation

5. If you leave no spouse or children or issue

All to the government

6. If you leave no lawful heirs

---

*   Plus household furniture and life interest in family home

** Children of deceased child (grandchildren) take that child's share

APPENDIX 6

RECORD KEEPING

PERSONAL INFORMATION

1. Your Name _____

    Address _____

    Telephone _____ Birth place _____

    Birth date _____ S.I.N./S.S. # _____

    Marital status _____ State of health _____

    Insurable?_____

2. Spouse's name_____

    Address _____

    Telephone _____ Birth place _____

    Birth date _____ S.I.N./S.S. # _____

    Marital status _____ State of health _____

    Insurable?_____

3. Children:

    Name   1 _____   2 _____

    Address   _____   _____

                    _____   _____

                    _____   _____

    Telephone   _____   _____

    Birth place   _____   _____

    Birth date   _____   _____

    S.I.N./S.S. #   _____   _____

    Marital status _____   _____

PERSONAL INFORMATION — Continued

3. Children — Continued

   Name   3 _____   4 _____

   Address   _____   _____

                          _____   _____

                          _____   _____

   Telephone   _____   _____

   Birth place   _____   _____

   Birth date   _____   _____

   S.I.N./S.S. #   _____   _____

   Marital status   _____   _____

4. Your parents:

   Names _____

   Address _____

   Telephone_____   Birth places _____

   Birth dates_____   Mother's maiden name _____

5. Spouse's parents:

   Names _____

   Address _____

   Telephone_____   Birth places _____

   Birth dates_____   Mother's maiden name _____

6. Next of kin:

   Name _____   Relationship_____

   Address_____   Telephone_____

7. Neighbor or close friend:

   Name _____   Telephone _____

   Address_____

ASSET DETAILS

1. Checking, savings, credit union, and other cash accounts

    Name of institution _____ _____ _____

    Type and number
    of account _____ _____ _____

    Interest rate _____ _____ _____

    Current balance _____ _____ _____

    Owned by _____ _____ _____

    Location of
    checkbook
    or pass book _____ _____ _____

2. Money market funds, certificates of deposit, and notes

    Name of institution _____ _____ _____

    Type and certificate
    number _____ _____ _____

    Maturity date _____ _____ _____

    Amount invested _____ _____ _____

    Interest rate _____ _____ _____

    Owned by _____ _____ _____

    Location of certificate _____ _____ _____

    Annual income _____ _____ _____

3. Securities

    Stocks and mutual funds:

    Number of shares _____ _____ _____

    Company _____ _____ _____

    Date purchased _____ _____ _____

    Cost _____ _____ _____

    Current market value _____ _____ _____

    Owned by _____ _____ _____

ASSET DETAILS — Continued

3. Securities — Continued

   Location of certificate _____ _____ _____

   Annual income _____ _____ _____

   Bonds: corporate and government

   Face Amount _____ _____ _____

   Company _____ _____ _____

   Date purchased _____ _____ _____

   Maturity date _____ _____ _____

   Total cost _____ _____ _____

   Interest rate _____ _____ _____

   Current market value _____ _____ _____

   Owned by _____ _____ _____

   Location of certificate _____ _____ _____

   Annual income _____ _____ _____

4. Real estate (residence, recreational, income property)

   Location _____ _____ _____

   Date purchased _____ _____ _____

   Cost _____ _____ _____

   Current market value _____ _____ _____

5. Life insurance

   Insured _____ _____ _____

   Company name _____ _____ _____

   Date policy issued _____ _____ _____

   Type of policy _____ _____ _____

   Coverage _____ _____ _____

   Current cash value _____ _____ _____

   Annual premium _____ _____ _____

PERSONAL CONTACTS

	Name	Firm name, address, and telephone
Lawyer	_____	_____
		_____
Accountant	_____	_____
		_____
Clergy	_____	_____
		_____
Stockbroker	_____	_____
		_____
Physician	_____	_____
		_____
Trust officer	_____	_____
		_____
Banker	_____	_____
		_____
Life insurance agent	_____	_____
		_____
Other insurance agents		
Homeowner	_____	_____
		_____
Automobile	_____	_____
		_____
Medical	_____	_____
		_____
Disability	_____	_____
		_____

PERSONAL CONTACTS — Continued

Executor of estate _____ _____

_____

Financial planner _____ _____

_____

Others _____ _____

_____

LOCATION OF OTHER IMPORTANT PAPERS

Homeowner's insurance _____

Name of company _____ Policy number _____

Automobile insurance _____

Name of company _____ Policy number _____

Medical insurance _____

Name of company _____ Policy number _____

Policy type _____

Location of card _____ Group number _____

Disability insurance _____

Name of company _____ Policy number _____

My will _____

Spouse's will _____

Codicils _____

Trust deeds _____

Birth certificates _____

Mortgage papers or lease _____

Deeds to real estate _____

Titles to automobiles _____

Military discharge papers _____

LOCATION OF IMPORTANT PAPERS — Continued

Citizenship papers _____

Divorce decree _____

Maintenance contracts _____

Social insurance/security number _____

Past income tax returns _____

Marriage contract or other agreement for property division _____

_____

_____

Details of property acquired in community property jurisdiction _____

_____

_____

Buy/sell agreement _____

Partnership agreement _____

Life insurance policies _____

Annuity contracts _____

Employment contract _____

Documents evidencing interest in employer's pension plan _____

_____

_____

Balance sheets and income statements for the last three years of all businesses in which I have a proprietary interest (either corporate, partnership, or proprietorship) _____

_____

_____

_____

_____

_____

REFERENCES

Better pensions for Canadians. Ottawa: Health and Welfare Canada, 1982.

Blotnick, Srully. *Getting Rich Your Own Way.* New York: Doubleday & Company Inc., 1980.

Bolles, Richard. *The Three Boxes of Life And How To Get Out of Them.* Berkeley: Ten Speed Press, 1981.

Brosterman, Robert and Thomas Brosterman *The Complete Estate Planning Guide.* New York: McGraw-Hill, 1987.

Brown, Kathleen H. *Personal Finance for Canadians.* 2nd ed. Scarborough, Ontario: Prentice-Hall Canada Inc., 1984.

Canadian Statistical Review. Ottawa: Statistics Canada, September 1984.

Catherwood, Robert H. *Your Money: How To Make The Most Of II.* 3rd ed. Toronto: Maclean-Hunter Limited, 1978.

Consumer Reports editors. *Your Retirement: A Complete Planning Guide.* New York: A & W Publishers, Inc., 1981.

Costello, Brian. *Your Money And How To Keep It.* Don Mills, Ontario: Stoddart Publishing, 1984.

Donoghue, William E. *Donoghue's Investment Tips for Retirement Savings.* New York: Harper & Row, 1986.

Duncan, Nancy. *Financial Savvy For Singles.* New York: Rawson Associates, 1983.

The Fiscal Plan. Ottawa: Department of Finance, May, 1986.

Goodman, Millie. "Checklist" *Canadian Tax Journal* Vol. 33, No. 3, Toronto: Canadian Tax Foundation, May-June 1985.

Hospital morbidity 1979-80 and 1980-81. Ottawa: Statistics Canada, 1984.

Hunnisett, Henry S. *Retirement Guide For Canadians.* North Vancouver: International Self-Counsel Press Ltd., 1987.

Kelman, Steven G. *Financial Times of Canada 1984 No-Nonsense Guide To RRSPs/RHOSPs And Other Tax Shelters.* Toronto: Methuen, 1983.

Lawson, James A. *Canadian Retirement Planner*. Toronto: Bessborough Publishing, 1984.

Lewin, Elizabeth S. *Your Personal Financial Fitness Program*. New York: Facts On File, Inc., 1983.

Life tables, Canada and Provinces 1980-82. Ottawa: Statistics Canada, 1984.

McIntyre, Harvey L. *A Practical Guide to Financial Planning for Retirement*. Life Underwriters Association of Canada, 1983.

McLeod, W.E. *Tax Shelters* 12th ed. North Vancouver: International Self-Counsel Press Ltd., 1987.

Ohmae, Kenichi. *The Mind of the Strategist; Business Planning for Competitive Advantage*. New York: McGraw-Hill, 1982.

Olive, David "Lapses and Collapses" *Report on Business Magazine*, Vol. 2, No. 3. Toronto: The Globe and Mail, September 1985.

Perry, Robert L. *The Financial Post Money Management Book*. Toronto: Maclean-Hunter Limited, 1976.

Report Of The Parliamentary Task Force On Pension Reform. Ottawa: Special Committee on Pension Reform, 1983.

Riehl, Gordon *Reduce Your Personal Taxes* Don Mills Ontario: General Publishing Co. Ltd., 1979.

Snyder, J. Christopher and Brian E. Anderson. *It's Your Money*. 3rd ed. Toronto: Methuen Publications, 1982.

Stub, Holber. R. *The Social Consequences of Long Life*. Springfield, Illinois: Charles C. Thornas Publisher, 1982.

Volker, Albert. *Save Tax in Canada and Retire at 45*. Don Mills, Ontario: Paperjacks, 1973.

Women and poverty: a report by the National Council of Welfare. Ottawa: National Council of Welfare, 1979.

Women In The Labour Force: Part 1, Participation. Ottawa: Labour Canada, 1983.

Wylie, Betty Jane and Lynne MacFarlane. *Everywoman's Money Book*. Toronto: Key Porter Books, 1984.

Zimmer, Henry B. *The New Canadian Tax & Investment Guide For Executives, Professionals & Business*. Edmonton: Hurtig Publishers Ltd., 1980.

CANADIAN
ORDER FORM
SELF-COUNSEL SERIES

NATIONAL TITLES   02/89

Asking Questions 7.95
Assertiveness for Managers 9.95
Basic Accounting 6.95
Be a Better Manager 8.95
Best Ways to Make Money 5.95
Better Book for Getting Hired 9.95
Between the Sexes 8.95
Business Etiquette Today 7.95
Business Guide to Effective Speaking 6.95
Business Guide to Profitable Customer Relations 7.95
Business Writing Workbook 9.95
Buying and Selling a Small Business 7.95
Civil Rights 9.95
Complete Guide to Home Contracting 19.95
Credit, Debt, and Bankruptcy 7.95
Criminal Procedure in Canada 16.95
Death in the Family 8.95
Design Your Own Logo 9.95
Editing Your Newsletter 14.95
Entrepreneur's Self-Assessment Guide 9.95
Environmental Law 8.95
Every Retailer's Guide to Loss Prevention ....
Family Ties That Bind 7.95
Federal Incorporation and Business Guide 14.95
Financial Control for the Small Business 6.95
Financial Freedom on $5 a Day 7.95
Fit After Fifty ....
For Sale By Owner 6.95
Forming and Managing a Non-Profit Organization
in Canada 12.95
Franchising in Canada 6.95
Fundraising 5.50
Getting Elected 8.95
Getting Started 10.95
How to Advertise 7.95
How You Too Can Make a Million in the Mail Order Business .. 9.95
Immigrating to Canada 14.95
Immigrating to the U.S.A. 14.95
Keyboarding for Kids 7.95
Landlording in Canada 14.95
Learn to Type Fast 11.50
Managing Stress 7.95
Margo Oliver's Cookbook for Seniors ....
Marketing Your Product 12.95
Marketing Your Service 12.95
Medical Law Handbook 6.95
Mike Grenby's Tax Tips 7.95
Mobile Retirement Handbook 9.95
Mortgages & Foreclosure 7.95
A Nanny For Your Child 7.95
Newcomer's Guide to the U.S.A. 12.95
Patent Your Own Invention 21.95
Planning for Financial Independence 11.95
Practical Guide to Financial Management 6.95
Practical Time Management 6.95
Radio Documentary Handbook 8.95
Ready-to-Use Business Forms 9.95
Retirement Guide for Canadians 9.95
Selling Strategies for Service Businesses 12.95
Small Business Guide to Employee Selection 6.95
Sport and Recreation Liability and You 8.95
Start and Run a Profitable Beauty Salon 14.95
Start and Run a Profitable Consulting Business 12.95
Start and Run a Profitable Craft Business 10.95
Start and Run a Profitable Restaurant 10.95
Start and Run a Profitable Retail Business 11.95
Starting a Successful Business in Canada 12.95
Step-Parent Adoptions 12.95
Taking Care 7.95
Teenagers and Suicide 8.95
Travelwise ....
Upper Left-Hand Corner 10.95
Wise and Healthy Living ....
Working Couples 5.50
Write Right! 5.50

PROVINCIAL TITLES

Divorce Guide
❏ B.C. 9.95 ❏ Alberta 9.95 ❏ Saskatchewan 12.95
❏ Manitoba 11.95 ❏ Ontario 12.95

Employer/Employee Rights
❏ B.C. 7.95 ❏ Alberta 6.95 ❏ Ontario 6.95

Incorporation Guide
❏ B.C. 14.95 ❏ Alberta 14.95 ❏ Manitoba/Saskatchewan 12.95 ❏ Ontario 14.95

Landlord/Tenant Rights
❏ B.C. 7.95 ❏ Alberta 6.95 ❏ Ontario 7.95

Marriage & Family Law
❏ B.C. 7.95 ❏ Alberta 8.95 ❏ Ontario 7.95

Probate Guide
❏ B.C. 12.95 ❏ Alberta 10.95 ❏ Ontario 11.95

Real Estate Guide
❏ B.C. 8.95 ❏ Alberta 7.95 ❏ Ontario 8.50

Small Claims Court Guide
❏ B.C. 7.95 ❏ Alberta 7.50 ❏ Ontario 7.50

Wills
❏ B.C. 6.50 ❏ Alberta 6.50 ❏ Ontario 5.95
❏ Wills/Probate Procedure for Manitoba/Saskatchewan 5.95

PACKAGED FORMS

Divorce Forms
❏ B.C 11.95 ❏ Alberta 10.95 ❏ Saskatchewan 12.95
❏ Manitoba 10.95 ❏ Ontario 14.95

Incorporation
❏ B.C 14.95 ❏ Alberta 14.95 ❏ Saskatchewan 14.95
❏ Manitoba 14.95 ❏ Ontario 14.95 ❏ Federal 7.95
❏ Minute Books 17.95
❏ Power of Attorney Kit 9.95

Probate
❏ B.C. Administration 14.95 ❏ B.C. Probate 14.95
❏ Alberta 14.95 ❏ Ontario 15.50
❏ Rental Form Kit (B.C., Alberta, Saskatchewan, Ontario) 4.95
❏ Have You Made Your Will? 5.95
❏ If You Love Me Put It In Writing – Contract Kit 14.95
❏ If You Leave Me Put It In Writing – B.C. Separation Agreement Kit 14.95

Interim Agreement
❏ B.C. 2.50 ❏ Alberta 2.50 ❏ Ontario 2.50

Note: All prices subject to change without notice.
Books are available in book and department stores, or use the order form below.
Please enclose cheque or money order (plus sales tax where applicable) or give
us your MasterCard or Visa number (please include validation and expiry dates).
✂--

(PLEASE PRINT)
Name _____
Address _____
City _____ Province _____
Postal Code _____
❏ Visa/ ❏ MasterCard Number_____
Validation Date_____ Expiry Date _____
If order is under $20.00, add $1.00 for postage and handling.
Please send orders to:
SELF-COUNSEL PRESS
1481 Charlotte Road
North Vancouver, British Columbia   V7J 1H1

❏ Check here for free catalogue.

SELF-COUNSEL PRESS INC.
ORDER FORM

NATIONAL TITLES　　　　04/89

_____	Aids to Independence	11.95
_____	Arrested! Now What?	7.95
_____	Asking Questions	7.95
_____	Assertiveness for Managers	9.95
_____	Basic Accounting	6.95
_____	Be a Better Manager	8.95
_____	Between the Sexes	8.95
_____	Business Etiquette Today	7.95
_____	Business Guide to Effective Speaking	6.95
_____	Business Guide to Profitable Customer Relations	7.95
_____	Business Writing Workbook	9.95
_____	Buying and Selling a Small Business	7.95
_____	Design Your Own Logo	9.95
_____	Entrepreneur's Self-Assessment Guide	9.95
_____	Every Retailer's Guide to Loss Prevention	15.95
_____	Exporting From the United States	12.95
_____	Family Ties That Bind	7.95
_____	Financial Control for the Small Business	6.95
_____	Financial Freedom on $5 a Day	8.95
_____	Fit After Fifty	8.95
_____	Franchising in the U.S.	6.95
_____	Fundraising for Non-profit Groups	5.50
_____	How You Too Can Make a Million in the Mail Order Business (Washington & Oregon)	9.95
_____	Immigrating to Canada	14.95
_____	Immigrating to the U.S.A.	14.95
_____	Keyboarding for Kids	7.95
_____	Learn to Type Fast	11.50
_____	Managing Stress	7.95
_____	Margo Oliver's Cookbook for Seniors	9.95
_____	Marketing Your Product	12.95
_____	Marketing Your Service	12.95
_____	Mobile Retirement Handbook	9.95
_____	Newcomer's Guide to the U.S.A.	12.95
_____	Parent's Guide to Teenagers and Suicide	8.95
_____	Planning for Financial Independence	11.95
_____	Practical Time Management	6.95
_____	Radio Documentary Handbook	8.95
_____	Ready-to-Use Business Forms	9.95
_____	Small Business Guide to Employee Selection	6.95
_____	Start and Run a Profitable Beauty Salon	14.95
_____	Start and Run a Profitable Consulting Business	12.95
_____	Start and Run a Profitable Craft Business	10.95
_____	Start and Run a Profitable Restaurant	10.95
_____	Start and Run a Profitable Retail Business	12.95
_____	Starting a Successful Business on the West Coast	12.95
_____	Taking Care	7.95
_____	Travelwise	7.95
_____	Upper Left-Hand Corner	10.95
_____	Wise and Healthy Living	9.95
_____	Working Couples	5.50

STATE TITLES — WASHINGTON AND OREGON

(Please indicate which state edition is required)

Divorce Guide
❑ Washington (with forms) 12.95   ❑ Oregon 12.95

Employer/Employee Rights
❑ Washington 5.50

Incorporation and Business Guide
❑ Washington 12.95   ❑ Oregon 11.95

Landlord/Tenant Rights
❑ Washington 6.95   ❑ Oregon 6.95

Marriage & Family Law
❑ Washington 7.95   ❑ Oregon 4.95

Probate Guide
❑ Washington 9.95

Real Estate Buying/Selling Guide
❑ Washington 6.95   ❑ Oregon 3.95

Small Claims Court Guide
❑ Washington 4.50

Wills
❑ Washington 6.95   ❑ Oregon 6.95

PACKAGED FORMS

Divorce
❑ Oregon Set A (Petitioner) 14.95
❑ Oregon Set B (Co-petitioners) 12.95
❑ If You Love Me — Put It In Writing 7.95

Incorporation
❑ Washington 12.95   ❑ Oregon 12.95

Probate
❑ Washington 9.95
❑ Rental Form Kit 3.95
❑ Will and Estate Planning Kit 4.95

All prices subject to change without notice.

✄ _

(PLEASE PRINT)

NAME _____

ADDRESS _____

CITY _____

STATE _____

ZIP CODE _____

Check or money order enclosed

If order is under $20, add $2.50 for postage and handling. Allow six weeks for delivery.

Washington residents add 8.1% sales tax.

Please send orders to:

SELF-COUNSEL PRESS INC.
1704 N. State St.
Bellingham, Washington 98225
❑ Check here for free catalog